how meaning relates to ideology, by touching on a wide range of contributions to that debate before offering her own suggestion.

The papers of the second part interpret a variety of specific texts in ways that illustrate the interplay of various theoretical approaches. Thomas Cartelli examines how the corrupt and unpolished text of Shakespeare's *Timon of Athens* has evoked a range of critical responses, from attempts to "improve" the text to explorations of the underpinnings of Shakespeare's dramatic art to dismissals of the play from sustained consideration. John C. O'Neal's essay discusses the approaches to and ultimate solution of the problems self-representation poses in the autobiographical works of Jean-Jacques Rousseau. Ross Pudaloff discusses a related point, Thoreau's composition of himself as a narrator. Considering Thoreau's strategy for dealing with sex in *Walden* and *The Maine Woods* Pudaloff argues that Thoreau "solved what had become the problem of sexuality in the nineteenth century by making it a feature of the world rather than a constituent of the narrative self." In the final essay of the volume Timothy Peltason joins the discussion of the relation of self and world by focusing on how the act of emergence is presented in Tennyson's early poems, "The Kraken" and "The Lady of Shalott." While these poems as cautionary fables expose "the difficulties and the dangers facing the self that would make its debut . . . at the same time they are exemplary acts of emergence, announcing the presence of a strong, new poet."

BUCKNELL REVIEW

Text, Interpretation, Theory

STATEMENT OF POLICY

BUCKNELL REVIEW is a scholarly interdisciplinary journal. Each issue is devoted to a major theme or movement in the humanities or sciences, or to two or three closely related topics. The editors invite heterodox, orthodox, and speculative ideas and welcome manuscripts from any enterprising scholar in the humanities and sciences.

This journal is a member of the Conference of Editors of Learned Journals

BUCKNELL REVIEW
A Scholarly Journal of Letters, Arts, and Sciences

Co-Editors
JAMES M. HEATH
and
MICHAEL PAYNE

Editorial Board
PATRICK BRADY
WILLIAM E. CAIN
STEVEN MAILLOUX
JOHN WHEATCROFT

Assistants To The Editors
DOROTHY L. BAUMWOLL
JANE S. LENTZ

Contributors should send manuscripts with a self-addressed stamped envelope to the Editor, Bucknell University, Lewisburg, Pennsylvania 17837.

BUCKNELL REVIEW

TEXT, INTERPRETATION, THEORY

Edited by
JAMES M. HEATH and MICHAEL PAYNE

LEWISBURG
BUCKNELL UNIVERSITY PRESS
LONDON AND TORONTO: ASSOCIATED UNIVERSITY PRESSES

Associated University Presses
440 Forsgate Drive
Cranbury, NJ 08512

Associated University Presses
25 Sicilian Avenue
London WC1A 2QH
England

Associated University Presses
2133 Royal Windsor Drive
Unit 1
Mississauga, Ontario
Canada L5J 1K5

The paper used in this publication meets the minimum requirements of the American National Standard for Permanence of Paper for Printed Library Materials Z39.48-1984.

Library of Congress Cataloging in Publication Data
Main entry under title:

Text, interpretation, theory.

(Bucknell review ; v. 29, no. 2)
Includes bibliographies.
1. Criticism—Addresses, essays, lectures.   I. Heath, James M.   II. Payne, Michael.   III. Series.
AP2.B887 vol. 29, no. 2   051 s [801'.95]   85-5893
[PN85]
ISBN 0-8387-5097-4 (alk. paper)

(Volume XXIX, Number 2)

Printed in the United States of America

Contents

Recent Issues of BUCKNELL REVIEW

Notes on Contributors

THOMAS CARTELLI: Teaches at Muhlenberg College. He has recently published articles on Shakespeare and Ben Jonson in *Theatre Journal, Centennial Review,* and *Renaissance Drama* and is in the early stages of a book-length study of Marlowe, Shakespeare, and the psychology of theatrical experiences.

MARJORIE COOK: Taught at Miami University in Oxford, Ohio. She contributed articles to *South Carolina Review, Notes on Contemporary Literature, Robert Frost: Centennial Essays II.* She was on the Advisory Board of the Robert Frost Society.

HENRY D. HERRING: Teaches at the College of Wooster. He has published several papers on psychological issues in literature and film, on Robert Penn Warren's fiction, and on Marlowe and Webster. An essay on conceptualization in literature forthcoming in *New Literary History.* Present project: a book on literature as cognitive creation.

VINCENT B. LEITCH: Teaches at Mercer University. His books include *Deconstructive Criticism: An Advanced Introduction,* and editions of Robert Southwell's *Marie Magdalens Funeral Tears* and the *Poetry of Estonia: Essays in Comparative Analysis.*

JOHN C. O'NEAL: Teaches at Hamilton College. Publications: "Morality in Rousseau's Public and Private Society at Clarens," *Revue de Metaphysique et de Morale,* 89 (janvier-mars 1984). "The Perceptual Metamorphosis of the Solitary Walker," *L'Esprit Createur, 24.*

TIMOTHY PELTASON: Teaches at Wellesley College. He has published *Tennyson: The Emergence of the Poet,* an account of Tennyson's career through the publication of *In Memoriam.*

ROSS J. PUDALOFF: Teaches at Wayne State University. Published studies on William Byrd of Westover *(The Southern Literary Journal)*, Jonathan Edwards *(Mosaic)*, and Richard Wright *(Studies in American Fiction)*.

MARY BITTNER WISEMAN: Teaches philosophy at Brooklyn College and the Graduate Center of the City University of New York. Published articles in *American Philosophical Quarterly, Ethics, Journal of Aesthetics and Art Criticism,* and *Philosophy and Literature.*

Introduction

LITERARY criticism has begun in recent years to take several distinguishable forms. Practical criticism, the new criticism, or formalist criticism focuses primarily on the text itself and has as its aim the production of commentary or interpretation. Literary history, contextual criticism, and biographical criticism look behind or around the text to examine the world that produced it, that its author reacted against, or that it passed through on its journey to the present reader. Literary theory, hermeneutics, or critical theory examines the art of interpretation itself and, in so doing, often replaces the literary text with a critical text that becomes the focal point for study.

The aim of literary theory may be modestly descriptive if its interest is to account for the ways criticism is done, or it may be more far-reaching when, for example, it entertains such questions as: Is criticism possible? What produces meaning? Is language able to examine itself? Some modes of critical theory, especially the version of the Frankfurt School, argue that critical theories are forms of knowledge that are distinctively reflexive and stand as models or guides for human action. As the language of criticism has become more difficult and the number of conflicting theories more extensive, metacriticism, or comparative criticism, has emerged as a recognizable genre. Here the attempt is to present, describe, interpret, and mediate between rival theories, sometimes to praise or condemn how criticism is done. Both the variety and the passion of literary criticism suggest its importance for humanistic study, whether or not one comes to agree with Harold Bloom and Richard Rorty that criticism has replaced philosophy in England and America as the most vital discipline in the humanities.

The essays that follow exhibit the variety and intensity of contemporary critical discourse. The essays in Part I are essentially theoretical and metacritical. They make explicit what is largely implicit in the essays in Part II, and they point to the

11

substrata of current literary theory in the writings of Nietzsche, Freud, Marx, and contemporary French thought, especially that of Barthes, Foucault, Derrida, and Paul de Man. Rather than assuming a self-contained environment for theoretical reflection, these essays are open and responsive to the international dialogue on the future of literary study. The essays in Part II turn to texts of Shakespeare, Rousseau, Thoreau, and Tennyson both to illuminate difficulties in those texts with contemporary theory and to test theory against the texts themselves.

James M. Heath
Michael Payne

BUCKNELL REVIEW

Text, Interpretation, Theory

Theory and Interpretation

Derrida's Assault on the Institution of Style

Vincent B. Leitch

Mercer University

> everything will blossom beside a deconsecrated tomb
> —"The Parergon"[1]

A new wave of translations of later Derrida texts—experimental, less "philosophical" works—is about to appear: *Glas* (1974), *Signéponge* (1976–77), *La Vérité en peinture* (1978), and *La Carte postale* (1980). From the later period we already have in translation *Spurs* (1973), *Limited Inc* (1977), and "Living On: *Border Lines*" (1979). Yet none of these experimental texts—in French or English—has played a decisive role in the development of deconstructive criticism in America. (The same can be said of Derrida's essays on pedagogy—all written after the early 1970s.[2]) These works are "unreadable." When the new books appear in translation, the American literary establishment will experience another assault on its sensibility.

Much of Derrida's work, early as well as late, seeks to transform the style of learned discourse: it approaches "unreadability." This feature of Derridean deconstruction is programmatic, not accidental. It involves disturbing the surface of traditional intellectual discourse as in the epilogue to *Writing and Difference* (1967), "Dissemination" (1969), "The Double Session" (1970) as well as in *Spurs, Glas,* and the other later texts already mentioned. The whole enterprise of transforming style is formulated and occasionally tried in early texts and carried out more systematically in later ones. Commentators, notably Geoffrey Hartman, have examined Derrida's lexical, phonetic, mor-

17

phemic, and syntactical peculiarities—his neologisms, puns, anagrams, and shattered sentences.[3] As time goes on, Derrida's texts become increasingly more allusive, fragmented, unconventional, and discomforting. Characteristically, the project of Derridean deconstruction assaults traditional canons of "acceptable style." Yet no one has isolated and carefully scrutinized the strategic links between the disturbance of the surface of the text and the deconstructive project to re-form philosophical analytics.

Looking back in 1975, Derrida notes that his assault on style has been evident for a long time. Here we encounter a self-conscious allegory in which Derrida confronts the institution of philosophy:

> From what I shall call, in order to proceed quickly, my position or my point of view, it was evident for a long time that the work in which I was engaged—let's designate it through algebra, at the risk of new misunderstandings, (affirmative) deconstruction of phallogocentrism as philosophy—did not belong simply to the forms of the philosophical institution. This work, by definition, was not limited to a theoretical or even cultural or ideological content. It did not proceed according to the established norms of a theoretical activity. By more than one feature and at strategically defined moments, it had to resort to a "style" inadmissible [irrecevable] for an establishment of academic reading . . . , inadmissible even in some places where one believes oneself away from the university. As we know, it is not always in the university where "academic style" dominates.[4]

The institution of philosophy, with its traditional forms, and the university, with its academic style, cannot "receive" Derrida's experimental discourse. Such writing is not aimed as usual and simply at theoretical, cultural, or ideological content; it does not adhere to institutional norms. Strategically, it adopts a different "style." Though addressed to a French group, this observation pertains as well to Derrida's American audience: the program to assault style has not been admitted into the institution of academic discourse or into the institutionalization of deconstruction. Scholarly presses have not published series of books in a Derridean mode, nor have scholars, including the avant garde, conceived of deconstruction itself as a systematic project to transform style. In this domain, Derrida's impact has been minimal.

Derrida's assault on style works at once on two fronts. First, he seeks to disrupt the conventional forms of written discourse and, second, he aims to develop a new "philosophical" analytics: Derrida tampers with traditional manners of discourse *and* modes of analysis. The entire enterprise of Derridean deconstruction can be conceived of as a project to transform style. The deconstruction of style is not limited to wrenching the surface elements of discourse; it attacks the "syntax" of traditional knowledge and thought. The celebrated "critique of logocentrism" is one aspect of this project; the other is the "split writing" that characterizes the discursive forms of Derridean texts. In this essay, I propose to (re)situate the Derridean project of (affirmative) deconstruction on the "ground" of style. I shall reconsider some familiar passages in the history of deconstruction in order to feature the transformation of style as the fundamental force motivating the project of Derridean deconstruction. What my rewriting of deconstruction seeks is not so much a new way to arrange "old" materials as a way to let Derrida's later texts influence his earlier more celebrated works.

On Recommending Change of Style

Instead of beginning as usual with Derrida's frequently cited essay "Structure, Sign, and Play in the Discourse of the Human Sciences," I want to start with "The Ends of Man," the first text of Derrida published in English. In this paper Derrida reexamines the fascination of philosophy with phenomenology. In particular, he focuses on the work of Sartre and its German backgrounds starting with Hegel, demonstrating that much is amiss and laying out directions for a new mission. Near the end of his discourse, Derrida sketches the options for a new, a *deconstructive,* "philosophy." He finds that a shift from the phenomenological line of Hegel-Husserl-Heidegger in favor of an emphasis on a Nietzschean perspective and practice is called for and already in progress. Suggestively, he concludes "it is perhaps a change of style that we need."[5]

When he later examines Nietzsche in *Spurs,* Derrida insists that "if there is going to be style, there can only be more than one" and that "writing must be in the interval between several styles."[6] These observations occur in a text devoted to "Nietzsche's Styles." A linkage persists and solidifies between "The Ends of Man" and *Spurs:* the move from phenomenology

to deconstruction, from Heidegger to Nietzsche as patron, requires a change of style, a shift from style to styles, from the
relative order, clarity, and precision of established style to the
mixed modes, parody, and double dealing characteristic of deconstructive "split writing." In place of Heideggerean illumination and unveiling will be Nietzschean dissemination and
aporia. Heterogeneity will replace homogeneity and the
monaural will become stereophonic. Not surprisingly, dual
speakers sound off in "Tympan," *Glas,* and other later texts.
Derrida tampers with the surface features of academic style—a
move that he early recommends in "The Ends of Man" under
the sign of Nietzsche and under the aegis of a new "philosophy": (affirmative) deconstruction.

The need to transform style underwrites the practice of
paleonymics, outlined by Derrida in 1971 and noticed rarely
since then by his commentators. Paleonymics constitutes one
tactic used in the assault on style, as does the more celebrated
move of putting concepts "under erasure." If we want to offer a
new understanding of an old concept—or to suggest any similar transformation of the past—we find it necessary precisely to
use old names from the past. Any such traditional name or
concept carries with it, inescapably, a system of predicates, a
chain of linked and structured elements. A disruption here
entails other and related displacements. Critical discourse, in
these circumstances, faces disarray. Derrida's tactic of paleonymy seeks programmatically to maintain "an *old name* in
order to launch a new concept."[7] The style of discourse, in the
project of paleonymics, courts calculated dislocation—duplicity.[8]

Derrida's manipulation of the term *écriture* is the most famous example of paleonymic maintenance and transformation: the concept of *écriture* is exemplary of Derrida's
earliest assault on style. As most of us now know, *écriture* names
writing but in a new sense. *Writing,* after Derrida's paleonymic
transformation, designates any fundamental process of differentiation, spacing, and inscription. In this sense, making a path
through a thicket, as much as penning a tract, enacts *écriture:*
spaces are opened, tracks are engraved, differences are produced. *Writing* here names not merely the traditional instrumental transcription of speech onto a page, but the primordial
production and recording of all differences, spaces, and traces.
By extracting *écriture* from its old system of predicates and ex-

tending it into other domains, Derrida sets going a deconstructive chain reaction: linguistics, metaphysics, and anthropology, as demonstrated in *Of Grammatology*, undergo severe questioning and criticism as their old systems of exclusion and inclusion and their particular objects and subjects of study are shown to be both arbitrary and groundless as well as phonocentric and logocentric. Without rehearsing further Derrida's notorious grammatological deconstructions of Western metaphysics, Saussurean linguistics, and structural anthropology,[9] we can see that the extraction and extension of old names, the production of such *undecidables* as *écriture* and the famous *supplément*—that the tactic of paleonymics—seeks a new, a double way of writing. Taking an old name, which is part of a traditional systematics, and altering that name's semantics outlines (the alteration is marked by italics), Derrida effects a disruption of the system and foregrounds potent dissymmetries. Rather than enrich the meanings of such key words, Derrida both uncovers and engenders radical uncertainties. Centers and hierarchies, dependent on such old concepts, are shaken—deracinated. Disturbing certain surface features and forms of discourse, Derrida begins to affect deeper structures—the syntax of things. In the project to transform style, deconstructive analytics plays a decisive role.

Progressively, the analytical program of Derridean deconstruction involves a continuous and insistent shift from terminology to rhetorical organization, from semantics to syntax. In place of meaning and truth are system and function. Derrida asks less "what is X?" or "what does X mean?" and more "how does X work in its particular field or system?" Thus Derridean deconstruction attends ever more closely to the *links* between concepts and their frames and boundaries as these produce inclusions, exclusions, and connections. Increasingly, joining elements, logical hinges, conceptual pivots, and discursive borders and margins constitute the materials of deconstructive analytics. The noun, pronoun, and adjective are less central and compelling than the conjunction, verb, and preposition. This is so because for Derrida relations and movements ultimately determine substances and qualities. Early in the game, deconstructive paleonymics enforced differential relations between old and new concepts. This "between," the opening of and for dissymmetrical connections, brings up disruption not merely on a local level but on the scale of system.

Whole conceptual fields are thrown off center. Thus, when Derrida recommends "writing must be in the interval between several styles," the stress on the *interval,* on the *between,* foregrounds the continual emphasis of deconstruction on the pivots and hinges, the syntax, of systems. Change of style involves transformation of both the surface and the syntax of learned discourse. Typically, commentators portray this double project as one-sided.

On Remarking Double Reading/Double Writing

Recommending change of style implicates a great deal more than we might first imagine. When he outlines paleonymics on the opening pages of his preface to *Dissemination* (1972), Derrida remarks that this tactic for handling old names "should give rise to a double reading and a double writing."[10] Change of style affects reading as well as writing. In effect, the whole matter of reading enters into the project to transform style. This linkage is already established in *Of Grammatology* (1967): "Because we are beginning to write, to write differently, we must reread differently."[11]

We can assay the Derridean reflection on reading in the exemplary essays of close reading collected in *Dissemination,* which were initially published between 1968 and 1970. Early in "The Double Session," for example, Derrida warns: "But a reading here should no longer be carried out as a simple table of concepts or words, as a static or statistical sort of punctuation. One must reconstitute a chain in motion, the effects of a network and the play of a syntax" (p. 194). Here the stress falls on links within and among systems, on networks and their syntax as opposed to emphasis on isolated concepts and terms or on points of arrest and punctuation. Not surprisingly, "The Double Session" is a doubled text that starts with a two-column page citing Plato on the left and Mallarmé on the right; it "finds its corner," as Derrida so emphatically indicates at the outset, "BETWEEN literature and truth" (p. 177). Here as elsewhere Derrida is less interested in one thing or another than in their connections and linkages, betweens and joinings. Substance and content—semantics and thematics—depend upon syntax. In "The Double Session," therefore, one reads less about "literature" and "truth" as such than about the strange *hymen* and *fold:* these undecidables, like Derrida's many others, track the gaps within the old logocentric system of critical concepts. Derrida ungrounds the system and its concepts. In the end the mysterious hymen and fold occupy the voided spaces of traditional poetic theories: mimetic, expressive, and didactic theories, tying "literature" to "truth," undergo deconstruction. This subversion of old beliefs happens by virtue of a *reading* of Plato and Mallarmé. Characteristically, Derridean reading reconstitutes an old conceptual chain in motion, isolating for scrutiny certain undecidable links and openings, folds and hymens; in such reading eccentric syntax comes to the surface and the surface of discourse becomes eccentric.

About midway through "The Double Session" Derrida reflects at some length upon "betweenness." His thinking starts with the enigmatic hymen but quickly expands outward, hinting at the broad scope of the project to transform style:

> The hymen in the text . . . is inscribed at the very tip of this indecision. This tip advances according to the irreducible excess of the syntactic over the semantic. The word "between" has no full meaning of its own. *Inter* acting forms a syntactical plug; not a categorem, but a syncategorem. . . . What holds for "hymen" also holds, *mutatis mutandis,* for all other signs which, like *pharmakon, supplément, différance,* and others, have a double, contradictory, undecidable value that always derives from their syntax. . . . Without reducing all these to the same, quite the contrary, it is possible to recognize a certain serial law in these points of indefinite pivoting: they mark the spots of what can never be mediated, mastered, sublated, or dialecticized. . . . Insofar as the text depends upon them, *bends* to them, it thus plays a *double scene* upon a double stage. [Pp. 220–21]

Derridean deconstructive analytics assiduously isolate for view syncategorems, betweens, which, by definition, are two-faced, contradictory, and undecidable. Mining and harnessing local manifestations of indecision, Derrida refuses any dissolution of terminal indefiniteness. Mediation, sublation, mastery, and dialecticization seem repressive operations, impositions of semantics on syntax, mechanisms fabricated to provide solace and protection, coherence and order. Each undecidable, each syncategorem or between—*supplément, différance, écriture, hymen*—has a local habitation and an old name. But each has a serial, systemic function and a new, mobile significance. Focusing on the structuration of systems or on the crossing points of networks, Derrida seeks to intervene and open destabilizing and permanent doubleness, continuous and irresolvable bifur-

cations. Strategically, his writing itself manifests such doubleness—sometimes in double columns, sometimes in paleonymic italics, and sometimes in other split formats.

As a reader, Derrida is epicure of the between and the split.
He illustrates how a text folds into and disseminates out of an
enigmatic, bifurcated node or, more typically, a series of such
nodes. Reading in this way and writing as such, Derrida, a
meticulous archeologist of traditional syncategorems, frequently employs the tactics of paleonymic double dealing: systematically, he maintains yet transforms old names. Taking up
classic texts of Western culture one after another, he insists on
the necessity of a painstaking doubled reading and writing.
Glas, the massive double-column text setting Hegel on the left
and Genet on the right, manifests most memorably the Derridean deconstructive manner, its duplicitous reading and writing.

Not only does Derrida examine numerous versions of betweenness, but he tries to occupy that space. He attempts to
lodge his own discourse in the between. In this effort, he seeks
not resolution but undecidability, not clarity but unreadability.
To avoid being thematized or categorized, the vigilant deconstructor constructs his own doubled text. In *Glas*, Derrida observes "if I write two texts at once, you cannot castrate me," and
in a nearby slim column he offers these revealing fragments:

> double posture.
> Double postulation.
> Contradiction in-
> itself of two irrec-
> oncilable desires.
> I present it here,
> imputed in my language,
> the style of DOUBLE
> BAND.[12]

Writing, deconstructive writing, courts contradiction in itself.
Style, in the old sense, is conciliatory. Deconstructive style, con-
versely, wants to be irreconcilable. Reading, in the old sense,
seeks to clarify the meaning and ethical value of texts; in the
new deconstructive sense, reading searches out and celebrates
contradictions and undecidables, turning up and aside simultaneously an arbitrary and one-sided, a masterful and exclusive,
system of valuation. *Glas*, according to Derrida, "is neither a

philosophical text, nor a poetic text; it circulates between these two genres, but while trying to produce another text, which is of another genre or which is without genre."[13] Inhabiting such "betweenness," *Glas* assaults genre itself.

Reading as well as writing, once again, "must be in the interval between several styles." The emphasis here falls heavily on the *interval*. Derrida aims not so much to enrich or pluralize discourse as to indefinitize it. Under the old regime, the terminally double, contradictory and undecidable as distinctive features of learned reflection and discourse find no place or warrant; they are inadmissible in the institution of learning.

On Reading Phenomenology in Quotation Marks

The shift from Heideggerean to Nietzschean, from phenomenological to deconstructive "philosophy," called for at the close of "The Ends of Man," requires change of style, to a new, a double, writing and reading. With Derridean deconstruction a general shift from semantics to syntax, from content to formation, from idea and substance to structure and system, from categories to syncategorems, from nouns to conjunctions, from relative certainty to radical indecision, from meaning and value to contradiction and undecidability, from order and hierarchy to their organization and fabrication, from logic to grammar, from a serious and sober discourse to a speculative and split poetics: a broad transformation of "philosophical" style gets underway.

The break of deconstruction with the philosophical institution, perhaps as abrupt as my syntax has tried to suggest, shows up most insistently in Derrida's early encounters with phenomenology—the last metaphysics dedicated to salvaging the remains of Western philosophy.

The general argument with phenomenology, articulated in detail in Derrida's *Speech and Phenomena* (1967) and in numerous other works, concerns the complicit notions of *presence, truth, voice, being* and *identity.* When Derrida looks into Heidegger or Husserl or Sartre, he localizes a recurring structural cluster or network in which, notably, existence or human being *(Dasein)* is determined as a being-present to itself. Inserting *différance* into this nexus, Derrida destabilizes the foundations of the phenomenological edifice—a house with many cells and passageways. Without recounting this well-known, manifold critique, one can summarize its effects by observing that Derrida regularly turns presence toward absence, identity toward difference, voice toward writing, and truth toward dissemination. In deconstructive terms, Derrida textualizes phenomenological discourse.

Such a reading of phenomenology produces certain alterations in our conventional understanding of reading and writing—of "philosophical" style. This new configuration appears most compactly in the elliptical *Spurs,* an enigmatic text that examines not only Nietzsche but, at midpoint, Heidegger on Nietzsche. Derrida's opening move is to impugn style (in the old singular sense of that word), for it typically "protects the presence, the content, the thing itself, meaning, truth,"[14] suppressing the inevitable absence of the thing, its dissemination and difference in writing. Writing, in the new manifold sense of *écriture,* dissimulates the "thing," puts it in *quotation marks,* inscribes it. What this tactical notation insists on is the double character of style: style is more a parodic replacement for an absent "thing" than it is single-minded monumentalization or embodiment of a thing's presence. The antagonist here is the traditional concept of "style" that lays claim to science, objectivity, or truth. To counteract the reign of these old values, the double character of "style" requires special emphasis—quotation marks, the tactical double strokes that appear everywhere in Derridean discourse.

According to Derrida's programmatic account in *Spurs,* it is Nietzsche who

> inaugurates the epochal regime of quotation marks which is to be enforced for every concept belonging to the system of philosophical decidability. The hermeneutic project which postulates a true sense of the text is disqualified under this regime. Reading is freed from the horizon of the meaning or truth of being, liberated from the values of the product's production or the present's presence. Whereupon the question of style is immediately unloosed as a question of writing. [P. 107]

Here we glimpse the importance, the historical significance, Derrida assigns to quotation marks. Following Nietzsche, his goal is to set all phenomenological concepts, particularly "meaning," "truth," and "being," in quotation marks. The deconstruction of these concepts, their submission to *écriture,* marked by quotation marks, doubles these concepts. For instance, there is truth and "truth." "The divergence within truth elevates itself. It is elevated in quotation marks . . ." (p. 57). This divergence, difference, or split doubles "truth," cutting its singular connections with "meaning" and "presence," "being" and "voice." The trajectory and outcome of this rereading and rewriting of phenomenology is the disqualification of hermeneutics: "The hermeneutic project which postulates a true sense of the text is disqualified under this regime."

In *Spurs*, as elsewhere, Derrida puts a handful of key phenomenological concepts into question. He manages this very often through quotation marks, the double marks characteristic of deconstructive discourse. The effect is to render the decidable undecidable. Hermeneutics, a deciding science, gets disqualified. And reading is freed from its ties to meaning, truth, presence and being. Style, as traditional medium of meaning and truth, likewise undergoes disqualification. In the deconstructive era, reading and interpretation are transformed into matters of writing and style; that is to say, in the new era, every term is both doubled and divided, written and rewritten. No longer are writing and style detours traversed by the cautious reader on the way to meaning and truth. The condition of detour is permanent and fundamental.

On Rereading/Rewriting Patrons, Practices, and Strategies

When the French text of "The Ends of Man" was published in 1972, it differed from the earlier English text. Where the English observes "it is perhaps a change of style that we need," the French goes on to say "and if there is style, Nietzsche reminded us, it must be *plural*."[15] Like *Spurs*, the updated text of "The Ends of Man" confers on Nietzsche's text, rather than Heidegger's, a certain position of eminence. The generic undecidability of this text, its general excess, as both Paul de Man and Jacques Derrida labored to show throughout the 1970s, serves as a model for deconstructive discourse. What *Finnegans Wake* is to the postmodern novelist, the work of Nietzsche is to the contemporary deconstructive theorist. However unlikely a patron, Nietzsche presides over the project of deconstruction. Not surprisingly, "Nietzsche" designates here not a man, but a mishmash of texts, plural styles, doubled writings and readings— epochal betweenness. In the hands of deconstruction, the old name "Nietzsche" is actively reread and rewritten—trans-

formed. What has happened is more a reversal than a revival:
phenomenological hermeneutics, the last humanism, submits
to the gay science. Accordingly, the between, where Heidegger
formerly located the gods, undergoes quotation marks and becomes the hollow space, the site of *différance*, where Derrida
localizes the division and doubling of all that is bounded and
bordered, the linguistic crossing point of all creation and production. Deconstruction transports our old names, concepts,
conventions, and texts across this divide, practicing between
styles of writing and reading. At the point at which this preposition "between" becomes an adjective, we court the possibility of
immobilizing the affirmative project to transform style.

The *change of style* Derrida calls for involves assaulting conventional manners of discourse and traditional modes of analysis; it affects practices of writing and reading. Style is "productive." How we know what we know results from style. What is
excluded from knowledge is a function of style as well. The
Derridean practices of paleonymics, of "quotation marks" and
of split formats, aim to double and render undecidable—to
make unreadable—the concepts as well as the texts of tradition
and of contemporary scholarship and criticism. The project to
transform style, conceived as an epochal shift, attacks directly
standards of prose and rules of genre as well as procedures of
analysis and conventions of understanding.[16] What style must
be for Derridean deconstruction is precisely improper and unreadable, intervallic and undecidable: style becomes frivolous
"double talk" or vice versa. "Order, clarity, precision: not only
does logic lack these, but writing too—the philosophical style.
Philosophical style congenitally leads to frivolity."[17] The assault
on the institution of style underlies the fundamental project of
Derridean deconstruction from the tactical use of quotation
marks to paleonymic italics, from puns to double bands, from
the focus on textual systems to the analysis of syntactical hinges
and betweens, from *Speech and Phenomena* and *Of Grammatology*
to *Glas* and *La Carte postale*. The deconstructive transformation
of style produces new practices of writing and reading—
transformed modes of discourse and analysis. Traditionally,
style occupies the margins of the philosophical institution; with
Derrida it comes to inhabit the "matrix."

Depending on the particular circumstances, Derrida may
present a text more or less "experimental," more or less "unreadable." On the occasion of assuming a visiting appointment

as Professor-at-Large at Cornell University in 1983, Derrida offered his first public lecture on the idea of the university. Here the assault on the institution of style becomes remarkably "readable": it is aimed at approving the future transformation not only of modes of analysis and manners of discourse but of forms of pedagogy and academic departmentalization. The entire university institution is Derrida's target. At one telling point Derrida criticizes radical sociology and psychology for submitting to the traditional analytics of science—the logocentric "principle of reason"—whereupon he suddenly turns toward the fundamental questions and then toward the basic strategies necessary today for the deconstructor *within* the university. Let us conclude with these three revealing moments:

[1] Whatever may be their scientific value—and it may be considerable—these sociologies of the institution remain in this sense internal to the university, intra-institutional, controlled by the deep-seated standards, even the programs, of the space that they claim to analyze. This can be observed, among other things, in the rhetoric, the rites, the modes of presentation and demonstration that they continue to respect. Thus I shall go so far as to say that the discourse of Marxism and psychoanalysis, including those of Marx and Freud, *inasmuch* as they are standardized by a project of scientific practice and by the principle of reason, are intra-institutional, in any event homogeneous with the discourse that dominates the university in the last analysis. . . . [E]ven when it claims to be revolutionary, this discourse does not always trouble the most conservative forces of the university. Whether it is understood or not, it is enough that it does not threaten the fundamental axiomatics and deontology of the institution, its rhetoric, its rites and procedures. The academic landscape easily accommodates such types of discourse more easily within its economy and ecology; [2] however, when it does not simply exclude those who raise questions at the level of the foundation or non-foundation of the foundation of the university, it reacts much more fearfully to those that address sometimes the same questions to Marxism, to psychoanalysis, to the sciences, to philosophy and the humanities. It is not a matter simply of questions that one *formulates* while submitting oneself, as I am doing here, to the principle of reason, but also of preparing oneself thereby to transform the modes of writing, approaches to pedagogy, the procedures of academic exchange, the relation to language, to other disciplines, to the institution in general, to its inside and its outside. [3] Those who venture forth along this path, it seems to me, need not set themselves up in opposition to the principle of reason, nor need they give way to "irrationalism." They may continue to assume *within* the university, along with its memory and tradition, the imperative of professional rigor and competence. There is a double gesture here, a double postulation:

to ensure professional competence and the most serious tradition of the university even while going as far as possible, theoretically and practically, in the most direct underground thinking about the abyss beneath the university. . . . It is this double gesture that appears unsituatable and thus unbearable to certain university professionals in every country.[18]

We have here, ironically, the clearest passage yet on Derrida's broadest conception of the deconstructive project. This statement summarizes two decades of a widening exposition and critique of logocentric analytics (*the* principle of reason) and of logocentric discourse (the rhetoric, rites, standards, and methods of learned "writing"). Here Derrida particularly criticizes "radical" Marxism and psychoanalysis for submitting to the principle of reason and complying with standard practices of academic discourse. These "disciplines" are comfortably at home in the institution; they do not raise questions about the (non)foundation of the university. Those who do formulate such questions—even when tactically they adhere to the principle of reason—face exclusion from or create fear in the institution. This is so because these questioners, "deconstructors," prepare the way to transform institutional procedures and practices—"academic style." For deconstructors within the university Derrida recommends a double strategy. First, deconstructors need not oppose the principle of reason or give way to irrationalism; they may maintain traditions and professional standards. This is a "paleonymic gesture." Second, deconstructors should go as far as possible, in theory and in practice, in thinking about the (non)foundation of the university and in working toward transformation of its "style." Derrida recommends an assault on the syntax as well as the surface of this institution.

Notes

1. Jacques Derrida, "The Parergon," trans. Craig Owens, *October,* no. 9 (Summer 1979), p. 40.

2. On Derrida's pedagogical writings, see my "Deconstruction and Pedagogy," *Writing and Reading Differently: Deconstruction and the Teaching of Composition and Literature,* ed. Michael L. Johnson and G. Douglas Atkins (Lawrence, Kans.: University Press of Kansas, 1985).

3. See, for example, Geoffrey H. Hartman, *Saving the Text: Literature/Derrida/Philosophy* (Baltimore, Md.: Johns Hopkins University Press, 1981), esp. chaps. 1, 2;

Hartman, *Criticism in the Wilderness: The Study of Literature Today* (New Haven, Conn.: Yale University Press, 1980), esp. chaps. 6, 8; and Barbara Johnson, "Derrida's Styles," which is the fourth section of the translator's introduction to Derrida's *Dissemination*, trans. B. Johnson (Chicago: University of Chicago Press, 1981), pp. xvi–xviii.

4. Jacques Derrida, "Où commence et comment finit un corps enseignant," *Politiques de la philosophie*, ed. Dominique Grisoni (Paris: Grasset, 1976), pp. 63–64; my translation.

5. Jacques Derrida, "The Ends of Man," trans. Edouard Morot-Sir et al. in *Language and Human Nature. A French-American Philosophers' Dialogue*, ed. Paul Kurtz (St. Louis, Mo.: Warren H. Green, 1971), p. 206. "The Ends of Man" was first published in *Philosophy and Phenomenological Research* 30 (1969): 31–57.

6. Jacques Derrida, *Spurs: Nietzsche's Styles*, trans. Barbara Harlow (Chicago: University of Chicago Press, 1979), p. 139. This text was given as a lecture in 1972 and first published in 1976 in Italy. At the end of his Postscripts, Derrida dates his text 1973.

7. Jacques Derrida, "Positions" [1971], *Positions*, trans. Alan Bass (Chicago: University of Chicago Press, 1981), p. 71. Derrida also outlines his tactic of *paleonymics* in "Signature Event Context," trans. Samuel Weber and Jeffrey Mehlman in *Glyph* 1 (1977): 195. This paper was read at a conference in Canada in August 1971 and published in Derrida's *Marges* in 1972.

8. Models of "duplicitous styles" for Derrida include especially texts by Artaud, Bataille, Mallarmé, and Sollers—all of whom he investigates in the 1960s. These writers attack both traditional philosophical conceptuality and discursive formats.

9. For an account of these celebrated deconstructions, see my *Deconstructive Criticism* (New York: Columbia University Press, 1983), esp. chaps. 1, 2.

10. Derrida, *Dissemination*, p. 4. Further references will be cited in the text.

11. Jacques Derrida, *Of Grammatology*, trans. Gayatri Chakravorty Spivak (Baltimore, Md.: Johns Hopkins University Press, 1976), p. 87.

12. Jacques Derrida, *Glas* (Paris: Galilée, 1974), p. 77; my translation.

13. Jacques Derrida, *L'Oreille de l'autre: Otobiographies, transferts, traductions—Textes et débats avec Jacques Derrida*, ed. Claude Lévesque and Christie V. McDonald (Montreal: VLB, 1982), p. 186; my translation.

14. Derrida, *Spurs*, p. 39. Further references are cited in the text.

15. Jacques Derrida, "Les Fins de l'homme," *Marges—de la philosophie* (Paris: Ed. de Minuit, 1972), p. 163. My translation of "et s'il y a du style, Nietzsche nous l'a rappelé, il doit être *pluriel*." Evidently, Derrida added these clauses to the earlier version of his essay.

16. In discussing the troublesome title of a Blanchot récit *L'Arrêt de mort*, Derrida indicates how, in general, "unreadability" functions in his assessment: "I maintain that this title is unreadable. If reading means making accessible a meaning that can be transmitted as such, in its own unequivocal, translatable identity, then this title is unreadable. But this unreadability does not arrest reading, does not leave it paralyzed in the face of an opaque surface: rather, it starts reading and writing and translation moving again. The unreadable is not the opposite of the readable." Jacques Derrida, "Living On: *Border Lines*," trans. James Hulbert, *Deconstruction and Criticism*, ed. Harold Bloom et al. (New York: Seabury, 1979), p. 116. What Derrida observes here about "unreadability" applies to his own texts. Tactically, "unreadability" forces redoubled reading.

17. Jacques Derrida, *The Archeology of the Frivolous: Reading Condillac*, trans. John P. Leavey, Jr. (Pittsburgh, Pa.: Duquesne University Press, 1980), p. 125.

18. Jacques Derrida, "The Principle of Reason: The University in the Eyes of Its Pupils," trans. Catherine Porter and Edward P. Morris, *Diacritics* 13 (Fall 1983): 16–17.

Constructivist Interpretation: An Alternative to Deconstruction

Henry D. Herring
College of Wooster

A S many practitioners and opponents have already claimed, deconstruction defies exact definition precisely because it interrogates whatever textual formulations confront it, including, instantaneously if possible, its own formulations. By finding the thread in each text to "unravel" it to "undecidability," in J. Hillis Miller's phrasing, deconstructionists relentlessly expose the "freeplay" that undermines our belief in "presence," "center," or "stability," because these tropes disintegrate, when tampered with, into "absence," the "*aporia*," the dizzying "*mise en abyme.*"[1]

In proposing an alternative theory focused on literary works, I will not attempt to refute deconstruction. I have been dizzied often enough by its "readings" to find its realization in practice unarguable. Instead, by sharing certain of its beliefs, such as the unnecessariness of single, fixed, determinate truth, especially in most spheres of human behavior or critical interpretation, and by rejecting others, particularly the notion that this lack of fixity destroys the possibility of knowledge (a space incongruously shared by E. D. Hirsch, Jr. and Paul de Man), I want to set out a different perspective in which variability functions not as deconstruction but as construction. I am calling this critical theory "constructivism" in order to emphasize the role of construction in cognitive processes. The term parallels frequent phrases such as "construction of reality" as used by cognitive psychologists whose research is crucial to the theory. Fundamentally, the contrast between deconstruction and constructivism that I want to make singles out two different critical goals that require divergent critical assumptions and practices—neither of them impossible, but one distinctly preferable to me.

On the one hand, deconstruction seeks an outcome of paralysis in its confrontation of the impossibility of certainty. This paralysis frequently comes disguised as motion in the incessant doubling back of texts on themselves so that emergence, development, and elaboration of them are "always already" precluded. Deconstruction is always on the move, but it never goes anywhere.

On the other hand, constructivist criticism seeks an outcome of knowledge (operationally defined here as structured conceptual complexes that integrate information into categories, formulate specific relations between them, and can be believed or accepted as a guide for human behavior). This knowledge, however surrounded it may be by uncertainty, grows out of constructions of conceptual and cognitive models that generate explanatory "fits" for existential complexity. This knowledge can be used to anticipate future events, to guide behavior, and to develop modified conceptions of social relationships. Yet, because uncertainty exists, because new information and experience will be encountered, and because the elaboration of concepts engenders variant concepts, constructivist criticism invites revision and modification as a process of active refinement and thus expresses no weariness at its necessity. One of my main contentions is that literature functions fundamentally as a conceptual, cognitive, and constructive medium that participates in the generation and variation of knowledge valid for use in making decisions and taking actions in the experiential world.

To clarify the crucial contrasts between the deconstructionist and constructivist positions, I first want to analyze some of Paul de Man's main arguments as representative of some recurrent positions in deconstructive practice, fully aware that no one person represents deconstruction. De Man's radically skeptical philosophy of language constitutes the crux in his writings that compels him to reject the possibility of acquiring meaningful knowledge.

In the earlier essays in *Blindness and Insight* and the later essay "Shelley Disfigured,"[2] de Man denies that literary language can be differentiated from ordinary language. Literary language embodies "the duplicity, the confusion, and the untruth that we take for granted in the everyday use of language" (*Blindness*, p. 9). More extremely, in "Shelley Disfigured," he argues that rhyme, however deliberately chosen it seems, may be "generated by random and superficial properties of the signifier rather than by the constraints of meaning" (p. 60). Consequently, a duplicitous but virtually autonomous language interposes itself between us and the nonlinguistic world of objects and even our own actions. Language not only mediates and distorts our knowledge but actually constitutes human reality because it pervades existence and subordinates all utterances to its systemic limits and differentiations. Because our cognitive comprehension of experience must submit to an inherently falsifying language as its instrument of investigation, knowledge is impossible (pp. 62–64). Language, the texture of existence, oscillates perpetually and indeterminately, making its interpretation "a Sisyphean task . . . without end and without progress" (*Blindness*, p. 11; "Shelley," p. 53).

De Man not only rejects knowledge, but connectedness of any kind. He writes that "nothing, whether deed, word, thought or text, ever happens in relation, positive or negative, to anything that precedes, follows or exists elsewhere, but only as a random event" ("Shelley," p. 69). Since no connections, a basic component of the conceptual complexes that constitute knowledge, can exist, de Man also dismisses knowledge as a motive for interpretation, for "no degree of knowledge" could assuage the "madness" of reading and interpretation that resides in "the madness of words." Human productivity, for de Man, is precisely a "product" of a system of "production" (language), never an interpretive strategy devised by human agency, a jejune idea that lingers incongruously in contemporary signification. Writing, reading, and interpretation are instead compulsive acts, mistaken only by the naive as "a source of value" (p. 68). Nonetheless, in *Blindness and Insight*, de Man does privilege literary expression, without irony, over other writing because literature calls attention to its own lies, for the realization that "sign and meaning can never coincide, is what is precisely taken for granted in the kind of language we call literary." He concludes that literature cannot mean and refer since the "truth emerges . . . of the true nature of literature when we refer to it as *fiction* . . . [which] asserts, by its very existence, its separation from empirical reality" (p. 17).

Despite the risks of positing a meaning for de Man, his writing sets forth three fundamental concepts: 1) all language deceives although literary language virtuously reminds us of its deceit by insisting on "the fallacy of unmediated expression" (p. 17); 2) knowledge is impossible because language, our cognitive instrument, always interposes itself as falsehood and distortion; and 3) concepts have no meaning because making connections constitutes the symptom of an inherently human madness. De Man sacrifices any claim by literature (or, logically, any human act or expression) to provide legitimate knowledge about the world. Literature is stripped of value as a means of providing knowledge valuable for engaging the complexities of human existence in the nonliterary dimensions of everyday experience.

One notable characteristic of de Man's expression needs comment as a transition to constructivist theory because it points precisely to the difference between accepting an existence of uncertain knowledge in need of frequent revision and despairing over this condition as one of Sisyphean futility. I refer to his absolutist language: for example, "it is the distinctive *curse* of all language, as soon as any kind of interpersonal relation is involved, that it is *forced* to ['hide meaning behind a misleading sign']"; "the *true nature* of literature"; "*nothing* . . . ever happens in relation . . . to anything that precedes, follows or exists elsewhere, but only as a random event" (emphasis added). Aside from the inconsistency of making such unequivocal claims from a philosophically skeptical position, they also represent, however inverted, efforts to do away with precisely the uncertainty that they are intended to reveal. If we know that language *must* deceive in interpersonal relations rather than knowing it *may* deceive if used deceptively, we may be discomfited, but we have defined with certainty the *nature* of interpersonal relationships, exactly as de Man has defined the "true nature" of literature and connection. In addition, the definition of interpersonal language as dishonest coincides with de Man's desire to remove agency and responsibility from language users and to place agency, at least, in language as a system. To reverse a slogan: people don't lie, language does.

In the position that I now want to elaborate, categorical thinking is much less appropriate. Because concepts, interpretations, and knowledge do not achieve finality, they are always open to alteration in an effort to discover better "fits" for the information, experiences, and purposes at hand. Nonetheless, they serve as our most adequate guides in the necessity of deciding and acting as we try to bring about configurations in the world that we presently believe to be desirable even though we are enmeshed in incomplete, uncertain, and changing knowledge—not only of the way things are, but of the way we might desire them to be—ways that often change even as we try to institute our desires. Thus, we may at least give up the anxiety of trying to insure that our constructions represent progress toward certainty and truth or lasting improvement since they are conceived of as the most probable or desirable ones presently available to us, but not as permanent.

Of course, we use other "models" or "constructions" all the time as "knowledge" for decisions and actions—"models" that constitute alterable, not permanent, conceptualizations of existence (neither copies nor mirrors) in physics, economics, or political science, for example. I am proposing that language, as literature, functions in multiple ways, one of them as a construction of conceptual complexes, a designation that will allow us to talk about literary fictions as a particular mode of generating knowledge, not as meretricious "lies" or as lies intended to prevent us from taking fictions seriously as de Man—and many who are not deconstructionists—would have it. Literary constructions stand parallel to, and interact with, other constructions of conceptual complexes that generate knowledge usable in the experiential world. Consequently, literature has a bond to action and responsibility.

One source for a better understanding of literature as creating usable knowledge can be found in pertinent research done in cognitive psychology. In these sources we can recognize that arguments for interpretive construction and the knowledge that arises from it need not be linked to the question of language alone. Some reasonably substantial evidence from investigations of cognitive processes in human development and behavior supports the idea that a conceptualizing, structuring process operates in human existence and has its beginnings prior to the development of linguistic competence.[3] Consequently, if the conceptualizing process precedes language and literature, then even if the process uses language (after competency) as its primary mode of implementation (not only by constructing concepts in speech and writing, but also in listening to or reading language, as Gerald Graff convincingly argues in "Literature as Assertion"),[4] the need to understand the conceptualizing activity in human experience becomes crucial. The indications are that, however much our conceptions might lack the durable meaning that de Man requires for them to have value or to meet his criteria of knowledge, we still use them to structure the ideas that we use as guides to action. Hence, the consequences of conceptual construction have enormous significance. In order to understand the connections between literary works, their interpretations, and their potential influence on human behavior, we will first need to look more closely at how constructions are used integrally in ordinary human functioning.

Cognitive psychology emphasizes the conscious and constructing capacities of human thought in learning, meaning, feeling, and behaving. Its theories have emerged from experimental studies; from investigations of cognitive development; from social psychology, especially the effect of causal attributions on human behavior; and finally, from clinical theories about belief systems in disturbed behavior. Clearly, this diverse range of evidence offers a broad epistemological grounding. To discuss these ideas as the basis for an alternative to deconstruction, I need to define two essential concepts: 1) the goal-orientation of action, and 2) the need to construct interpretations of experience. After that, I will set forth some initial elements of a constructivist literary theory.

The basic tenet of cognitive psychology holds that a person selects behaviors to achieve goals (or to solve problems or to bring about expected results). Essentially, this premise means that actions represent more complex decisions than can be accounted for by describing them as fully determined responses to preceding stimuli or to following reinforcers, such as electrical shocks, parental rewards, reading novels, or even deploying language systems. Although many such factors may influence behavior, the choice of an action (even though partially contingent on learning and situation) arises from the individual's judgment (leaving aside questions of skill or effectiveness) of the relationships between the desired goal and such matters as the value of the goal, the effort required to achieve success, and the probability that available strategies will work. Thomas Lidz anchors this pattern of decision and action in the person's ability to project himself purposefully into the future.[5] Constructivist thought posits both agency (the ability to choose and act efficaciously, not to choose uniquely and entirely free of contingency) and the projected expectation of a conceptualized future. This projected future is not dogmatic, unrevisable, or certain, but it is capable of being conceptually imagined as a focalizing device in the selection of strategy and action. This desire induces the individual to acquire, structure, test, and use information that he thinks will have value.

The second and most important characteristic of the cognitive/constructivist theory posits that human beings actively structure the information they encounter. Ulric Neisser and most other cognitive researchers conclude that human beings, in order to function, select and order the overwhelming volume of information they constantly receive into patterns that will be useful to them, excluding information that seems irrelevant. As Thomas Lidz stresses, a severe inability to form concepts leads to a total disorganization of the individual that brings functioning to a halt (pp. 59–63), the opposite position from de Man, who invites the disorganization of "disconnected" existence.

In general, then, the cognitive processes order, but, more significantly, the individual acquires, construes, structures and tests information to shape an interpretation of experience, or more accurately, integrates information into the construction already in place. This construction is then used to explain existence and to enable choices that will lead to completed goals. According to Jean Piaget, the individual, throughout his lifetime, uses cognitive skills for adaptation by assimilating elements of the external world to his present activities and also by accommodating his activities to the requirements of the surrounding world. The second major cognitive function comes with the acquisition of symbolic and structuring powers: the organization of experience. Beginning with simple acts like subordination (grasping comes to be understood as a component of pulling), the child moves to more complex and inclusive structurings of the knowledge required to achieve what is valued.[6] For Piaget, who conceived of his ideas as structuralist, the structure neither comes from predetermined sources nor remains fixed, but is being "constructed" all the time because of the continual processes of adaptation and organization that force the individual to "restructure" previous models into modified ones.[7] For Piaget, however, the unceasing reinterpretations do not evoke de Man's Sisyphcan futility of knowing. Instead, restructuring moves one toward more effective functioning or understanding.

George A. Kelly, another theorist, concludes, more specifically, that we structure experience to gain knowledge with which to predict (or at least gauge) the outcome of events, thereby enabling us to act with some assurance even though we almost always have imperfect knowledge. Kelly argues that a person generally tries "to improve those contructs through experience or education" in order to get better "fits" between what he expects to happen and what happens.[8]

Constructivist theory, then, fundamentally claims that an individual (or collectivity) actively generates a construction of the world (however correct or incorrect) based upon complex and constantly evolving sets of information, events, and concepts that he tests in multiple ways. The person uses this construction to make decisions and to act until it needs to be altered, perhaps because of a failed expectation that revealed a weakness in the construct. In any event the experiential model undergoes continuous modification from the interplay between expectations and outcomes. Ideally, from this process, a construction of experience evolves that constantly refines a person's knowledge into an effective, generative, but permeable guide to be used experientially in varying situations and as modified goals or different problems emerge.

These constructivist propositions describe a complex system of interlocking and interacting elements that rarely take identical shapes in each individual. The intricacies of the theory become clear in the effort to understand an individual's construal of the world and how it connects to his actions. This effort encounters many complications, some of which include determining the particular constellation of important experiences that an individual has had, differentiating processes of thinking that he has developed independently from the ones he has adopted as a result of the instructions of others, identifying the intermix of ready-made meanings that have been handed-on by the culture and that may be wholly unexamined, noting the conclusions that have been reached previously and routinized into virtually automatic premises for actions, and uncovering the interpretations that have been left incomplete or stand in contradictory relationships to other interpretations that may be held simultaneously. The cognitive approach to understanding the human mind, its thoughts, its feelings, and its role in actions demands a rigorous examination of human learning and behavior, both mental and physical.

Nothing in the perspective presented here denies to language and literature an extraordinarily important role in cognitive construction and functioning. Language, like any other internally consistent system, such as Euclidean or Riemannian geometries, may be most efficiently described in terms of its internally consistent, rule-governed structures that prevent it from copying anything other than itself. However, language may also function—perhaps less efficiently and precisely—to refer to (that is, to imply or to suggest or to call to mind or to deflect toward) that which is other than itself (entities, experiences, or concepts generated in language) in a way that parallels the use of different geometries to organize (imperfectly) spatial relations differently. Certainly cognitive psychologists acknowledge the crucial role of language in shaping our conceptions of experience into provisional coherence. Jerome Bruner, for one, not only cites language as our primary tool for organizing experience, but he also believes literature serves as one of the important "modes of knowing" because it uses language to create models of connectedness in experience.[9]

The potential diversity of cognitive interpretations might be taken as confirmation of the oscillating uncertainty on which de Man insists. However, the constraints on cognitive constructions need to be understood. In *Cognition and Reality*,[10] Ulric Neisser takes up this problem. Although individuals create "schema" that give them understandings of the world that allow them to act, Neisser rejects the contention that these interpretations can efficaciously explain the world in whatever terms that individuals, singly or collectively, desire. Because the external world does exist, however mediated it may be by perception (or language), it constrains the variations or arrangements that are both possible and effective for an individual's purposes, although he may choose the "fit" among the variants that most satisfies him, such as Ronald Reagan's preference for "user's fee" instead of "tax."

In the models of both Neisser and Piaget, cognitive constructions constantly interact, especially through action, with externalities. These interactions are precisely the reasons that individual (and collective) schema must undergo continuous, partial revision. The individual must encoutner and—in Piaget's terms—partially assimilate to his operating construals of experience objects, events, people, and other interpretive schemes (including those in literary works) that exist externally to himself, but he must also accommodate himself to them. The cycle thus begins with the person's current constructions of his world, continues with the taking of actions (or, importantly, I would add, encountering new information in the act of reading a literary work) that then cause assessment of his construct as a result of what happens, and concludes with the maintenance or modification or possibly abandonment of the construction currently held (Neisser, pp. 20–23, 144). Because these external existents escape to some degree (a variable dependent on too many factors to describe here) the control and determination of the schema, it remains permeable and alterable, thereby increasing its capacity to anticipate changing circumstances and to achieve effective results. Although the full case cannot be argued here, this recognition of elements (notably, literary works) that are independent of, but neither controlling nor wholly controlled by, the perceiver places constraints (but not rigid controls) on literary interpretations as well—in contrast to the autonomous reader or restricting peer group of reader-response criticism in the versions, for example, of Norman Holland or Stanley Fish[11] and in contrast to the intertextual associationism of deconstruction. Consequently, constructivist thought offers a much better theory, in behavior and in literary interpretation, for avoiding the entrapment of the hermeneutic circle of self-confirming actions or interpretations since they must be corroborated by external encounters and measured by the attainment of goals or the solving of problems. Cognitive constructions, then, are conceptual schemes that give shape to multiple and complex experiences, and they are cognitive tools that enable us to determine what we accept as knowledge substantial enough to use as the basis of actions.

The evidence suggests that generating concepts represents a

commonly shared human activity designed to lead to a comprehension of the experiential world for the purpose of taking
effective action toward the achievement of goals in that world.
Although de Man may regard efforts to gain understanding as
meaningless or mad, his statements propose values that privilege lengthy duration, permanence, or transcendence as genuine knowledge. His deconstructionist position ignores an adequate explanation of how people continue to think, feel, and
act in uncertainty, with only provisional knowledge, but with
genuine commitments that have real consequences.

Paul de Man and other deconstructionists, though certainly
not alone, especially during the last two centuries, deny to literature the powers of conceptualization, the creation of credible
knowledge, and the legitimacy of actions based on literature.
However, because the implications of his premises extend to
cognitive models other than literature, de Man must also deny
as valid the evidence that suggests an enduring and effective
use by human beings of conceptualization to provide knowledge. Constructivst theory, on the other hand, reaches two
major, contrasting conclusions. Humans conceptualize to use
information efficiently, but they go further and construct inter-
pretational systems that enable them to evaluate experience
and to act.

Literature, I believe, can be more plausibly interpreted as a
manifestation of these cognitive capacities for structuring existence and gaining useful knowledge of it. Consequently, I now
want to transfer the significance of cognitive theory to literary
thought. Most importantly, literature has a valuable cognitive/
constructivist purpose rather than a role as merely a pleasing
aesthetic artifact or a comfort or an unbounded field of indis-
criminately disseminated signifiers—a few of the limiting roles
assigned to it in modern critical systems. Literature as a model
for constructing valid knowledge about the world has many
potential functions in a constructivist perspective. The following are just three of the possibilities: 1) to provide an imaginative working out of the genuine complexity of individual and
cultural beliefs about the world; 2) to set forth an imaginative
version of an altered world; and 3) to demonstrate the literary
work's correspondence to the human act of constructing experience.

In an effort merely to be suggestive rather than comprehensive, I will focus on how the literary work itself—in its creation

and in its reading—corresponds to the cognitive/constructive act. Albert Rothenberg, a psychoanalytic investigator, has reported that literary creation resembles the complexity and careful development found in secondary process thinking (the conscious and the rational in the Freudian scheme) much more than it does primary process thinking (the unconscious and the intuitive).[12] His findings reverse not only Freudian but many commonly held expectations. Constructivist theory, however, with its focus on adaptation and organization as processes consciously moving toward an informing interpretation of experience, would predict just this creative pattern. Literature, in its intricate orderings of form and content, serves as it seems to serve: first, to gain control over its selected materials and order them more coherently than in experience; and second, to construct them into one or several conceptual models revelatory of reduced, clarified, and patterned configurations referable to and usable in existence, although these models are neither existence itself nor its imitation. The literary work functions as a first-order cognitive interpretation, an initial but still densely saturated conceptualization of existence. However, especially as readers, we refine the literary construction further, condense it (or parts of it) critically into a secondarily created but additionally reduced and clarified construction that impinges upon our current model of existence, activating a reconsideration and potential alteration of our present beliefs and behavior.

Conceived from the perspective of constructivist theory, the literary work takes on a serious role. It effects a construct of beliefs that interpret the world with variable degrees of nomothetic or idiosyncratic emphasis, but it then elaborates, explains, validates and/or refutes the construct it creates through the ensemble of formal and substantive elements of which it is composed. Literature, then, need not be taken as a comfort or as a language construct that constitutes a unique entity set apart from existence or other forms of knowledge. Because the literary work, in constructivist theory, exists as an entity external to its creator and reader, neither totally dominant over nor dominated by an "other" (texts, linguistic conventions, authors, readers), and because it functions itself as an "other," an external model of existence not capable of absolute independence but incapable of simple reduction to the reader's model, it can confront our cognitive constructions with its own, grapple with and shape human thought and behavior by offer-

ing knowledge that alters our guiding conceptual constructions. Literature, itself a construction in a modality of fiction,
provides knowledge about how we build models of our world,
what the configurations of different models might be, how they
interact and conflict with one another, and how as human beings we continually adjust and revise them.

This reconception of the function of the literary work does
not deny the validity of other ways of conceiving literature. For
example, while it may not emphasize a work's aesthetic functions, it not only accepts them, but even acknowledges the shaping powers of form as an integral component in determining
the construction of existence offered by the work.

Constructivist criticism as practice focuses on the cognitive
strategies created in the work—discerning their main lines and
their points of intersection with other systems of belief in the
work, determining the directions of change, and assessing the
effectiveness of a character or speaker's construct from within
his conception of his world. Constructivist criticism may also
add conceptual refinement and elaboration, especially perhaps
to emergent versions of the world that a poet may be imaginatively constructing, as in Adrienne Rich's meticulously cognitive
re-visioning and restructuring throughout her work of how
women might come into existence in the world.

In conclusion, I will return to goals. In constructivist theory,
the mode of literature is fiction, but literature is a cognitive
construction, parallel to economics, for example, that yields
conceptual knowledge capable of belief and use in ordinary
experience. As experientially usable knowledge, literature must
be open to interaction with other fields of knowledge, accepting
and offering appropriately interactive corroboration. Given
these assumptions and conditions, the primary goal of a constructivist theory can be explored: the elaboration of the knowledge available in literature for responsible experiential action.
Even though literary knowledge, like all other knowledge,
often points to multiple (not limitless) means for attaining
goals; even though it probably never achieves certainty; and
even though it may validly move us toward goals that we then
alter, these limitations, though requiring continual reinterpretations and restructurings, do not deny knowledge and thus do
not pull us toward the self-indulgent dizziness of the deconstructionist abyss. These reinterpretations become precisely the
maneuvers that generate modified knowledge to be used anew

in action; to be used to bring about what we perceive presently, but not permanently, as desirable change; to be used to conceptualize our futures. Deconstruction ends with confusion and paralysis, a sophisticated unraveling of despair. Constructivism elaborates, varies, changes, and points toward action in the world, a process sustained by an unending extension of human conception and cognition.

Notes

1. J. Hillis Miller, "Walter Pater: A Partial Portrait," *Daedulus*, no. 105 (Winter 1976), p. 112; and "Stevens's Rock and Criticism as Cure: II," *The Georgia Review* 30 (Summer 1976): 341. Other essential works in the emergence of deconstruction, and especially of the terms noted in the text, are the first part of Miller's essay on Wallace Stevens in *The Georgia Review* 30 (Spring 1976); Paul de Man, "Political Allegory in Rousseau," *Critical Inquiry* 2 (Summer 1976); and Jacques Derrida, "Structure, Sign, and Play in the Discourse of the Human Sciences," *The Languages of Criticism and the Sciences of Man: The Structuralist Controversy*, ed. Richard Macksey and Eugenio Donato (Baltimore, Md.: Johns Hopkins University Press, 1970); and J. Derrida, *Of Grammatology*, trans. Gayatri Chakravorty Spivak (Baltimore, Md.: Johns Hopkins University Press, 1976), esp. pp. 1–95.

2. Paul de Man, *Blindness and Insight: Essays in the Rhetoric of Contemporary Criticism* (New York: Oxford University Press, 1971); and P. de Man, "Shelley Disfigured," *Deconstruction and Criticism* (New York: Seabury Press, 1979). All subsequent citations will be to these editions and will appear in the text.

3. Some valuable sources that discuss the existence and use of concepts prior to the development of language or in nonlinguistic forms after language acquisition include M. H. Bornstein and W. Kessen, eds., *Psychological Development from Infancy* (Hillsdale, N.J.: Lawrence Earlbaum, 1979); and L. S. Vygotsky, *Thought and Language*, ed. and trans. Eugenia Hanfmann and Gertrude Vakar (Cambridge, Mass.: The M.I.T. Press, 1962), pp. 42–43, 49–51. None of these investigators denies the prominence of language as competency is gained, but they argue that structured thought and action precede language acquisition.

4. Gerald Graff, "Literature as Assertion," *American Criticism in the Poststructuralist Age*, ed. Ira Konigsberg (Ann Arbor, Mich.: University of Michigan Press, 1981).

5. Thomas Lidz, *The Origin and Treatment of Schizophrenia* (New York: Basic Books, 1973), pp. 22, 53. All subsequent citations will be to this edition and will appear in the text.

6. Jean Piaget and Barbel Inhelder, *The Psychology of the Child*, trans. Helen Weaver (New York: Basic Books, 1969); these ideas are discussed in a number of places, but see especially pp. 4–6 and 153–59. All subsequent citations will be to this edition and will appear in the text.

7. Jean Piaget, *Structuralism*, trans. Chaninah Machsler (New York: Basic Books, 1970), p. 119.

8. George A. Kelly, *A Theory of Personality* (New York: Norton, 1963), p. 9.

9. Jerome S. Bruner, *On Knowing: Essays for the Left Hand*, expanded ed. (Cambridge, Mass.: Harvard University Press, 1979), pp. 59–60.

10. Ulric Neisser, *Cognition and Reality: Principles and Implications of Cognitive Psychology* (San Francisco, Calif.: Freeman, 1976), passim. All subsequent citations will be to this edition and will appear in the text.

11. Norman N. Holland, *Five Readers Reading* (New Haven, Conn.: Yale University Press, 1975); and Stanley Fish, *Is There a Text in This Class?* (Cambridge, Mass.: Harvard University Press, 1980).

12. Albert Rothenberg, "The Unconscious and Creativity," *Psychoanalysis, Creativity, and Literature: A French-American Inquiry,* ed. Alan Roland (New York: Columbia University Press, 1978), pp. 144–62.

Texts of Pleasure,
Texts of Bliss

Mary Bittner Wiseman

Brooklyn College

Only one language grows more and more contemporary: the equivalent, beyond a span of thirty years, of the language of *Finnegans Wake.*

It follows that the literary avant-garde experience, by virtue of its very characteristics, is slated to become the laboratory of a new discourse (and of a new subject), thus bringing about a mutation, "perhaps as important, and involving the same problem, as the one marking the passage from the Middle Ages to the Renaissance."

S O writes Julia Kristeva in a 1971 essay on the work of Roland Barthes,[1] whose aim she correctly maintains is to specify the key role of literature in the system of discourses. He does this by giving center stage to the notion of writing: " 'Literature' becomes *writing;* 'knowledge' or 'science' becomes the *objective formulation of the desire to write,* and their interrelationship (sets) the stakes where the subject is—within language through his experience of body and history."[2] Kristeva suggests that the originality of Barthes's work lies in the double necessity that literature be regarded from the viewpoints of the sciences of language, the body, and history at *the same time* and that the scientific approaches to literature be controlled by "the discreet and lucid presence of the subject of this 'possible knowledge' of literature, by the *reading* that he gives of texts today, situated as he is within contemporary history."[3]

In the early 1970s Barthes came increasingly to emphasize

47

the values of plurality, intertextuality, productivity of meaning, and the infinity of languages; as a result he came to attach less importance to the sciences of the subject and more importance to the subject's performance in reading. The performance is likened by Barthes in *The Pleasure of the Text* (1973) to the weaving of a piece of Valenciennes lace; to the act of love, where the creation of meaning is the climax of love, bliss, and the suggestion is strong that meaning lasts but a moment, as ecstasy does, and is purchased at the price of self, as ecstasy is; and to a costlier weaving than the weaving of lace:

> *Text* means *tissue;* but whereas hitherto we have always taken this tissue as a product, a ready-made veil, behind which lies . . . meaning (truth), we are now emphasizing, in the tissue, the generative idea that the text is made, is worked out in a perpetual interweaving; lost in this tissue—this texture—the subject unmakes himself, like a spider dissolving in the constructive secretions of its web.[4]

I want to see what sense can be made of this notion of the subject by looking at certain passages in *S/Z* (1970), an account of reading a Balzac short story, "Sarrasine," and *The Pleasure of the Text.*

Barthes distinguishes the traditional and the avant-garde texts in the following way:

> Text of pleasure: the text that contents, fills, grants euphoria; the text that comes from culture and does not break with it, is linked to a *comfortable* practice of reading. Text of bliss: the text that imposes a state of loss, the text that discomforts (perhaps to the point of a certain boredom), unsettles the reader's historical, cultural, psychological assumptions, the consistency of his tastes, values, memories, brings to a crisis his relation with language.[5]

The fact of the existence of the avant-garde text makes a demand on readers, and the fact that the demand is met by the development of a new mode of reading teaches a lesson about how meaning is produced. The demand is that readers *do something* to make sense of the text, for the text, if passively approached with the customary beliefs about the relations between literature and life, and words and world, is nonsense. The custom of the Cartesian is to make truth a supreme value resident in the reference of a representation (signifier) to what is represented (referent), where the reference is mediated by the concept (signified) of the represented object. The conceptual scheme in play is one whose deepest cut is between objective world and subjective self, with language handmaiden to the world it represents and the self whose thoughts and feelings it expresses. Speech and writing are instruments whereby speaker and writer make public their already-formed beliefs and intentions, but the palm goes to speech for presenting directly what writing, the record of speech, presents indirectly. What this view of language implies for literature is that literature copies the world and the passions and actions of its inhabitants, and authors speak to readers indirectly through their works—unless, that is, they have the artistry that Ford Madox Ford attributes to William Henry Hudson. Ford says of Hudson that it is impossible to tell how he got his effect, and when you read his books "you forget the lines and the print. It is as if a remotely smiling face looked up at you out of the page and told you things. And those things become part of your experience."[6]

The expectations spawned by the traditional ways of looking at literature are that the reader can position himself within the text by assuming the roles and, hence, adopting the points of view of, variously, author, narrator, and characters, and that what will appear from these positions is something recognizable as belonging to his world. These expectations are manifestly thwarted by the "Nighttown" sequence in James Joyce's *Ulysses*, for example, a cacophony of many different discourses "uttered" by characters whose descriptions, shape, sex, and appearance change so frequently that it is impossible to assign an origin to the utterances. Impossible, that is, to assign them to speakers conceived of as the Cartesian conceives of them: creatures substantial and enduring, consistent and integral, transparent to themselves, untouched by history, part of the original furniture of the world.

The challenge of the literary avant-garde cannot be met as were similar challenges to received thought posed by abstract art and non-Euclidean geometries: the one changed the conception of paintings from copies of the seen world to realities in their own right; the other changed the conception of geometry from a realistic description of actual space to a conventional description of some possible space. What is shaken by the avant-garde text are not simply beliefs about the relation of literature to what is outside it (including the relation of author and characters to reader), but, as Barthes registers in his characterization of the text of bliss, the reader's assumptions about the *world,* its past, its culture, and its people, his *self-*consistency, and his relation to *language.* The challenge of avant-garde literature reaches as far as language reaches: to linguistics, psychoanalysis, history, theories of culture; to the practices of self-identification and self-justification; in short, it moves throughout the system of discourses, with the result that these kinds of questions intrude themselves: can the world be regarded from the points of view of the different sciences and practices developed and developing in this century at *the same time?* Can the human subject be viewed through such different optics at the same time? If no to both, or either, what sorts of reasons can there be for privileging one point of view? In what language can a theory authorizing reasons for choosing among theories be couched? If there can be one metalanguage, why can't there be several, and if there are, how choose among them? If there can be a metalanguage, there can be a meta-metalanguage, and so on, endlessly.

Mimesis gives way to semiosis. To discover how the semiosis works, one must become like the writer, "someone for whom language is a problem, who experiences its profundity, not its instrumentality nor its beauty."[7] This describes the reader who in struggling to make something of the modern text discovers how language works in it and, a fortiori, how language works everywhere, even in the classic text and ordinary discourse, whose meanings seem to be ready made. It is not reasonable to suppose that there is a break in language and that its meanings are fixed except when it is used by the avant-garde writer: if the meanings of language *are* fixed, then no modern writer can wrench them from their "words" and no reader can make anything of the writers' efforts. But readers and writers conspire in producing the avant-garde text.

Writerly Reading

When Barthes reads the Balzac story "Sarrasine" in the way developed in response to the modern text, no violence is done to the story because it turns out that for any text to be intelligible it must have some measure of plurality, that is, it must be such that it *can* be read in what Barthes calls the "writerly" way.

S/Z begins with the observation—Barthes is always gentle—that the structuralist enterprise of trying to see all the world's stories within a single structure is undesirable because stories from which a model is extracted *lose their difference.* This difference whose loss is so to be regretted that Barthes will read in a wholly new way rather than suffer it, is defined by contrast with the familiar difference whereby texts are complete ("finished off"), individual, different from each other. To regard texts in light of this traditional difference is to place them in a "demonstrative oscillation, equalizing them under the scrutiny of an indifferent science, forcing them to rejoin . . . the Copy from which we will make them derive."[8] The oscillation begins with preanalytic intuitions about which particulars are similar enough to yield a single model and then moves to the particulars being "proved" to be instances of the extracted model by being derived from it. The best case is when the oscillation is stilled in reflective equilibrium. Then science and ideology have done their work: the models have been derived and described, and readers of nature or culture or books in which they appear need only match what is seen or read with its counterpart in the pantheon of models in order to understand what is seen or read. Such readers *consume* what science and ideology have wrought. Because the particulars that we confront in experience can be schematized in various ways, that is, can be viewed through the lens of the various sciences of our modernity, because there is no natural and, hence, no compelling way to classify, because we cannot theorize our mastery, it is well that we do not regard texts in light of their traditional differences.

What difference then? For with no difference nothing can appear. The desirable difference is such that texts seen in its light are not complete, not individual, not different from each other. To say that texts are not individual is to say that just as one copy of *Finnegans Wake*, although a different physical object from another, is not an individual, for novels do not consist in paper and ink, so "Sarrasine," although a different string of signs from *Finnegans Wake,* is not an individual, for texts do not consist in given strings of signs. Signs are relations between signifiers (sounds or inscriptions) and singifieds (concepts); when the concept associated with a sound or inscription changes, the sign changes. The acoustic or visible marks do not change, but such marks by themselves are noises or scribbles. Signs by themselves have no meaning; their meaning consists in the *syntagmatic* relations they have with the signs that come before and after them and the *paradigmatic* oppositions between them and the signs that might have been used in their stead.

Syntagms are possible verbal contexts or strings of signs; paradigms are sets of possible occupants of given positions in a syntagm; they are relations of difference: the meaning of a sign is a function of what it is not. Texts may be represented as networks of their horizontal syntagms and vertical paradigms, each intersection marking the site of a value of the texts' variable signs. To call signs variable is to say that in lieu of anything that might serve to fix the conjunction of signifiers and signifieds there is a shifting of signifiers "over" the signifieds of their horizontal and vertical neighbors, and a shifting of signifieds "under" their neighbors' signifiers. Cultures tend to try to fix the relation between signifiers and signifieds, and then, constant conjunction creating the impression of necessity, as David Hume saw and so forcefully showed, argue the necessity or naturalness of the relation. But a productive reading has the effect of performing a Humean demystification of the alleged naturalness of the customary relations between marks and their "meanings."

The textual network is complex and open in that, for example, one member of a paradigm to which a given sign belongs itself belongs to other paradigms, and the sign's recalling the one member opens the way to that member's recalling members of the other paradigms to which it belongs, and so on, endlessly. Texts may be said not to be complete because of the essential openness of the network of their signs. These signs recall, finally, or would recall to a language-omniscient reader (or a computer), the vast network of signs that is language. (More exactly, a text recalls its language [*langue*], and each language recalls language [*langage*] as the condition of its possibility.) So far as texts do refer to the whole of language, they are not different from each other.

To judge texts according to the difference within is "to restore each text, not to its individuality, but to its function, making it cohere, even before we talk about it, by the infinite paradigm of difference, subjecting it from the outside to a basic typology, to an evaluation."[9] Science does not evaluate, and culture reflects evaluations already made. The evaluation, the decision about how to regard texts, comes from the reader. In the opening pages of *S/Z* Barthes shows what he takes to go without saying, namely, that what is most to be valued is that the reader should have more than the poor freedom to accept or to reject a text, he should have the freedom to *produce:*

> On the one hand, there is what it is possible to write, and on the other, what it is no longer possible to write: what is within the practice of the writer and what has left it: which texts would I consent to write (re-write), to desire, to put forth as a force in this world of mine? What evaluation finds is precisely this value: what can be written today (rewritten) today: the *writerly.*[10]

The reference here to both what it is possible to write and what one would consent to write may seem puzzling, for one can hardly consent to write what is impossible. However, the impossibility is indexed to persons as well as to time, so that "impossible to write" is always "impossible for person P to write at time t," and what is or is not possible for a person is a function of how one positions oneself with respect to the sciences and ideologies of one's time.

What can be written is what can be *interpreted*, where interpretation is not finding the text's meaning but appreciating the plural that constitutes the text. Interpretation is an operation performed on a text that reveals "the more or less each text can mobilize." Imagine now a text that is absolutely plural and one that is not plural at all. For the first:

> posit the image of a triumphant plural unimpoverished by any constraint of representation (or imitation). In this ideal text, the networks are many and interact without any one of them being able to surpass the rest; this text is a galaxy of signifiers, not a structure of signifieds; it has no beginning; it is reversible; we gain access to it by several entrances, none of which can be authoritatively declared to be the main one; the codes it mobilizes extend *as far as the eye can reach,* they are indeterminable (meaning here is never subject to a principle of determination, unless by throwing dice); the systems of meaning can take over this absolutely plural text, but their number is never closed, based as it is on the infinity of language.[11]

When this text is read, some systems of meaning take it over for the moment of the reading, no matter how lightly the reader makes the assignment of values that he makes. To read is perforce to limit the plurality of the infinitely plural text; one can trace meanings *only* as far as one's eye can reach.

Imagine, against this, a text whose words have meaning not in their relations with other words but with essences, ideas, or behavior, in short, with some language-independent reality. Suppose that it is the only text in its language and, therefore, cannot be interwoven with other texts. (Nor can it be translated. Translation would require putting the meaning-conferring realities into language, and were that done, the linguistic expression of reality would replace reality in the new language. But that would violate the hypothesis that the text's words depend solely on what is outside.) Such a text can be understood only on the assumption that its meaning is given without remainder by the reality to which it is supposed to refer. The implications of this assumption have been worked out in detail in Wittgenstein's *Tractatus Logico-Philosophicus,* an account of how propositions, which are expressible in language, might be said to "mirror" reality. It demonstrates the impossibility of ever being able to say what the mirroring relation is and accedes to the impossibility with the admonition, "Whereof one cannot speak, thereof one must be silent." Moreover, it applies the inexpressibility of the allegedly meaning-conferring relation to the very propositions in which Wittgenstein has shown the inexpressibility: "My propositions are elucidatory in this way: he who understands me finally recognizes them as senseless, when he has climbed out through them, on them, over them. (He must so to speak throw away the ladder, after he has climbed up on it.)"[12] The impossibility of saying how language might be connected with nonlanguage infects language itself: we cannot even *say* that we cannot say how it is related to its other. Therefore, there is no language in which we can formulate the supposition that there is a text whose meaning is completely given by a determined and determining reference to the world, a text that is perfectly readerly, that is, consumable.

Might there not, however, be a text in which there is no plural because its meanings are given by fixed and single relations to other words? This absolutely readerly text could hardly be read in any sense of "read" worthy of the name. It could only be gazed at, and the gazing *at* would soon become a gazing *through* as a world crystalized on the other side of the gradually forgotten lines and print, a world in which were heard voices telling things to whoever was listening. And who would be listening were those who yielded to the impression that the customary conjunction between signifiers and signifieds is necessary, and so far as they have let themselves yield they have consented to the impossibility of their interpreting the readerly text.

What is ordinarily called reading is often passively consuming worlds and voices presented by culture and author; it is merely a kind of looking and listening. The other sort of reading is *operating* a text, speaking *to* it as to the other as instigator, as Kristeva says. A text can be operated only so far as its meanings are not tied down; a text in no wise thought to be constituted by systematic differences must be thought to be made up of stable meanings, which by virtue of being stable cannot be operated.

Here are two examples of Barthes operating on "Sarrasine." He breaks the text into reading units that may be words, sentences, paragraphs, or parts thereof and recombines or associates them by *codes*. Meanings are generated in "Sarrasine" by five codes: two are horizontal or syntagmatic (the hermeneutic code of question and answer and the proairetic code of actions); three are vertical or paradigmatic (reference codes relate elements to bodies of knowledge, the symbolic code relates elements as symbols, the semic code clusters signifiers into persons, places, or objects). The first example works through the semic code. Semes are connotation-rich signifiers, where connotations are secondary meanings whose signifiers are not acoustic or visible marks, but signs, which themselves signify characteristics or attributes. The final "e" in Balzac's title connotes femininity in French and is therefore related to all else that connotes femininity, whether or not the other signifiers appear in the text. Whereas the readerly reader will try to organize the semes within a text, either grouping them to form a character (or object or place) or arranging them into a thematic grouping, Barthes trades on the fact that what femininity signifies is uncertain, approximate, and unstable and allows the seme the "instability, the dispersion, characteristic of motes of dust, flickers of meaning." The second example uses the symbolic code. The word *daydream* in the first sentence of the story, "I was deep in one of those daydreams," lays the ground for the symbolic structure of the antithesis by uniting the adversatives "day" and "dream" in one word which is, then, joined not only to the antitheses introduced in the story's opening paragraph (salon and garden, life and death, heat and cold, inside and outside), but also to all other antitheses. The word *daydream* and the antithesis of salon and garden are "footprints marking the escape of the text . . . ventures out of the text, the mark, the sign, of a virtual digression toward the remainder of a catalogue (the *Kidnapping* refers to every kidnapping ever written); they are so many fragments of something that has always been *already* read, seen, done, experienced; the code is the wake of the *already*."[13]

The text is always already written, decodable only so far as encoded, and the code is the wake of the already. How then can the reader be said to be functioning in following the codes? How is he doing anything that a computer might not do? Put into a computer the vocabulary (the network of signs) and the formation and transformation rules of the reader's language, and the five codes through which Barthes read "Sarrasine." Put Balzac's text into the computer and instruct the machine to compile the indefinitely long lists of "references" the signifiers in the text make to each other and to the signifiers to which the codes connect them. The "references" are made via what the signifiers signify, but what they signify is a function of what in the text has gone before and will go after, of what other values could take their place, of what other values could appear in other positions of their syntagms, of what codes pass through the values that are or could be nearby. The computer's lists may be displayed as networks of possible meanings, too complex no doubt to be read by all but a language-omniscient reader, but this simply means that a computer can run through more possibilities than a person can, not that the person *does* anything in reading the text different from what the computer does.

The computer-generated network is not meaningful, however, for "meaningful" is always "meaningful-to." The move from displaying a text as a network of meanings to making it meaningful to its reader involves doing what a computer cannot do: unmake itself, "like a spider dissolving in the constructive secretions of its web." The computer cannot write. It cannot dissolve in the blissful achievement of meaning.

The Subject of Bliss

The experience of meaning consists in the dissolve of the reading subject into the fault, the seam, the edge between tradition and modernity. The redistribution of language that occurs in the avant-garde text, Barthes says in *The Pleasure of the Text*, is:

> *always achieved by cutting.* Two edges are created: an obedient, conformist, plagiarizing edge (the language is to be copied in its canonical state, as it has been established by schooling, good usage, literature, culture), and *another edge,* mobile, blank (ready to assume any contours), which is never anything but the site of its effect: the place where the death of language is glimpsed. These two edges, *the compromise they bring about,* are necessary. Neither culture nor its

destruction is erotic; it is the seam between them, the fault, the flaw which becomes so.[14]

This is precisely the distinction between texts of pleasure, in which language is obedient, and of bliss, in which language has emptied itself of its customary meanings and in which, therefore, the reader cannot find comfortable assumptions about world, self, and language. The fault between the two sorts of text exists only in the reader:

> Now the subject who keeps the two texts in his field and in his hands the reins of pleasure and bliss is an anachronic subject, for he simultaneously and contradictorily participates in the profound hedonism of all culture (which permeates him quietly under cover of an *art de vivre* shared by the old books) and in the destruction of that culture: he enjoys the consistency of his selfhood (that is his pleasure) and seeks its loss (that is his bliss). He is a subject split twice over, doubly perverse.[15]

Barthes uses throughout *The Pleasure of the Text* the language of film, talking as he does of "cuts" and "dissolves." They are different, of course, and I think that he uses them in such a way that cuts are more nearly logical and dissolves more nearly phenomenological. In the passage just cited there is a *cut* between traditional and modern texts and the kind of reading they invite: the conceptual frameworks presupposed by the old and the new are incompatible. The blissful *dissolve* is the effect of reading the modern texts, or of reading any texts in the modern, writerly way.

The first split that occurs in one who reads in the writerly way is the split between enjoying and seeking to destroy his culture and his selfhood. It is clear that one can be culture's child and enjoy the culture and the conception of the self that it puts forth without seeking to destroy it. However, one cannot try to destroy something that one does not in some way or other accept. The reader of the modern text must somehow have in mind the values of the traditional text in order to be able to hear the modern text "speak against" them. For if the new text does not speak against (contra-dict) something, it speaks into a vacuum and can be heard by no one. The writerly reader must have in mind also the values of the new, or he could not read in the writerly way. The reading subject becomes a "living contra-diction," enacting on the stage of his mind the drama of a culture in the throes of change.

When the beliefs that have shaped a culture are being replaced, they linger on as traces in the new, for the new beliefs are formed in the atmosphere of the old and bear their press, even when they are formally incompatible with the old. Until the old beliefs are forgotten, the culture may be said to be in danger of vanishing into the seam between the two. (Equally well-evidenced and widely accepted sets of incompatible beliefs simply cannot be contained within one culture: either one wins the day or the culture is split into two.) But once the old are forgotten the culture is in the greater danger of slipping back into the comfortable practice of supposing that its beliefs are natural, justified by nature or by the nature of things, and losing the lesson of the brief moment between the reigns of old and new: that beliefs are arbitrary, for there is no independent real correspondence with that which makes them true.

Consider now not all of culture but only the conception of the self that it holds dear: the conception of the self as *one*, in which deep splits constitute madness and less deep splits disorders to be remedied. The reading subject becomes a living contradiction by both believing that he is some one consistent thing and trying to cease to be what he believes himself to be. The experience of avant-garde literature contradicts the reader's customary way of regarding himself; if he does not regard himself in tradition's way, there is nothing for the new text to speak against and it cannot be heard. If, however, the reader cannot entertain the contradiction of his beliefs about himself, the avant-garde will be nonsense to him. The reader must, that is to say, entertain both the conventional beliefs about what he is and the contradiction of these beliefs. Moreover, to deny tradition's values once they have been unsettled by the modern text is to abolish the *differential value* of the modern: unless one believes in more than conventions, one must allow that the avant-garde has value only so far as it is different from what went before it. For the subject to appreciate the differential value of the new and the plurality it opens up, he must experience the value. He must, that is, not merely know *that* thus and so are the traditional beliefs about language, literature, self, and world that are unsettled by the modern text; he must *adopt the point of view* of one who accepts these beliefs. (This is a stance almost inevitable before the moment of our modernity and troubling after it.)

So far as the reader regards himself as one who adopts tradition's point of view, he cannot make anything of the modern text. This is just to say, however, that he cannot read the new text in the old way, where reading in the old way is really gazing at what shines through the lines and the print. When one looks at the avant-garde text through tradition's lens, nothing is in clear enough focus to make out. We may say the reader sees nothing. And when the reader does make something of the modern text, he has adopted the point of view of one who rejects the beliefs against which the sheer existence of the new as something that can be read speaks. Among the old beliefs that it speaks is the belief that there is something behind the print: a world in which the reader can locate himself, an author's voice with which the reader can identify. In giving up these beliefs about literature (in adopting the point of view of one who gives them up), the reader, if he is thoroughgoing, gives up belief in a world in which he may ever find himself and in voices he may pretend are his. The reader lives in the language and it, not an author, speaks to him. But, again, this notion is meaningful just in case the notion of there being a world full of speakers is meaningful. The first split in the "subject split twice over" is a rupture in the set of his beliefs: he believes there is a world full of speaking selves, including himself, and he believes that worlds and selves are but functions of the infinite play of language.

The second split is a fragmentation, a scattering, a pluralizing, that occurs in the course of writerly reading. It seems, however, that it is the text and not the subject which is undone by the reading. Any one text is:

> entrance into a network with a thousand entrances; to take this entrance is to aim, ultimately . . . at a perspective (of fragments, of voices from other texts, other codes), whose vanishing point is nonetheless ceaselessly pushed back, mysteriously opened: each single text is the very theory (and not the mere example) of this vanishing, of this difference which indefinitely returns, insubmissive.[16]

Think now of the sciences of the twentieth century from whose viewpoints literature may be regarded: linguistics, psychoanalysis, sociology, history. Each provides a perspective on the reading subject as well, and when one regards the subject from the viewpoints of the various sciences at the same time, there is a certain pluralizing of the subject. For example, the independence of the subject is challenged by the Marxist thesis that the subject is a function of the material means available to satisfy his material needs, and the power of the subject over itself is diminished by the Freudian discovery that what moves him is what he cannot know. The one theory connects the subject essentially with history, as it had not been thought to be connected, the other separates the subject from what had formerly been thought to be its own. The point is that when the contemporary sciences are seen in light of the traditional theories they speak against, and when the subject is seen within the redrawn boundaries of the subject, different sciences drawing the boundaries in different ways, there is a certain play. Each new system defines a perspective whose lines of sight one follows, only to find its vanishing point ceaselessly pushed back. What vanishes is the point that would fix the world, or the subject matter of the science, forever. No one fixed point will do. It might be remarked, however, that what is destabilized and set into play by the contemporary sciences is the *concept* of the subject, not the subject.

The avant-garde text makes us "think against" received theories and invites us to read the old theories as we have learned to read the new texts. Try now to read the traditional theories of the human subject in the new way. Follow all the codes through and out of the theories to other theories, other texts; listen to all the voices, even those heard murmuring offstage; read slowly, decomposing what is read. Since the subject is intelligible to itself only in terms of some theory, it is impossible for it to think itself along the lines drawn by a theory it interprets in a writerly way. For the subject would think its own dissolution as it dissolved the theory of itself. Even so, what is dissolved is the *theory* of the subject, not the subject.

Although the subject cannot think itself as plural, it does not follow that it cannot write itself, for writing is more like *performing* than it is like thinking. The question whether the reading subject can "perform" itself seems different, nonetheless, from the question of what happens to it as it performs *Finnegans Wake* or "Sarrasine." Barthes speaks of the subject's dissolving into the text as it reads and so far as this happens there is no logical distance between subject and text, and the subject's performance of the text *is* his performance of himself. What is this? The customary connections between signifiers and what they signify are wrenched apart, and the subject's commitments to the received doctrines of his culture (the *doxa*) are undone—the subject is wrenched from his "tastes, values, and memories."

Signifiers, at bottom, sounds and inscriptions, and readers, reduced now to bodies, the equivalent of the sounds and the visible marks that are signifiers, float free. There is a sense in which signifiers and readers are nothing, they are surely not significant, until concepts are attached to the perceptible marks, and objects (objects of thought, intentional objects) are attached to the reader's attitudes. There are many intentional objects (concepts) with which to bind signifier and reader, but there is no reason, no grounding gesture, to authorize assigning any one rather than another. The reader, therefore, choreographing his dance through the network of signs that is the text (whatever text he is reading), positions himself now here, now there, where each positioning, each step, is the summoning of some system of meaning that will for as long as the step lasts, bind signifier and reader. In the absence of any reason for stopping here rather than there, the reader/dancer will not stop at all. And so far as a subject is identified by his tastes, values, and memories, by the objects of his attitudes, by the contents of his mind, the writerly reader is not identifiable at all. No sooner has he adopted one point of view and one set of attitudes, than he has slid through some logical vacuum to another point of view, another set of attitudes. This fall through empty space is the collapse or the fall of the self of which Barthes speaks. This is the fragmentation of the self that is the second split in the subject "who keeps the two texts in his field and in his hands the reins of pleasure and bliss."

The accession to modernity signaled by a penchant for reading in the writerly way might seem to be accession to the value of plurality and the consequent devaluing of binary opposition, and we might be inclined to say of the cut between tradition and the modern that issued in the value of the plural that "we must throw away the ladder, after we have climbed up on it." But we cannot. One reason for this is that the value of plurality lies precisely in its undoing the traditional unity of signifier and what it signifies and the unity of self and a consistent set of attitudes. Another reason is that, as Barthes says: "Neither culture nor its destruction is *erotic;* it is the seam between them, the fault, the flaw which becomes so" (emphasis added). Barthes, like Socrates, knows the connection between eros and thought.

Notes

1. Julia Kristeva, "How Does One Speak to Literature?", *Desire in Language,* ed. Leon S. Roudiez (New York: Columbia University Press, 1980), p. 92. (Kristeva is quoting from Barthes's *Critique et vérité,* p. 48.)

2. Ibid., p. 94.

3. Ibid.

4. Roland Barthes, *The Pleasure of the Text,* trans. Richard Miller (New York: Hill and Wang, 1975), p. 64.

5. Ibid., p. 14.

6. Ford Madox Ford, *Portraits from Life* (Boston: Houghton Mifflin Company, 1980), p. 47.

7. Roland Barthes, *Critique et vérité* (Paris: Editions du Seuil, 1966), p. 46.

8. Roland Barthes, *S/Z,* trans. Richard Miller (New York: Hill and Wang, 1974), p. 3.

9. Ibid.

10. Ibid., p. 4.

11. Ibid., p. 6.

12. Ludwig Wittgenstein, *Tractatus Logico-Philosophicus* (London: Routledge & Kegan Paul, 1922), p. 189.

13. Barthes, *S/Z,* p. 20.

14. Barthes, *The Pleasure of the Text,* pp. 6–7.

15. Ibid., p. 14.

16. Barthes, *S/Z,* p. 12.

Meaning in Poetry: The Logic of Discovery

Marjorie Cook

Miami University

ITERATURE may abandon the truth-conventions to which
persons ordinarily are bound in communication, and it
adds an aesthetic convention, a concern for the beauty of the
work—when produced as "literature" by either author or
reader.[1] These definitive characteristics of literature have been
emphasized in this century in ways that make meaning in literature problematic: literature's being aesthetic seems to
minimize, even eliminate, the referential function of its language, and its being fictional seems to preclude its being knowledge. For these reasons, much current criticism focuses only on
literature's structural patterns. Poetry as the most formal of the
literary genres is particularly vulnerable to these current emphases on structure. In this paper we will see that the emphases
on structure with a concomitant elimination of reference in
poetry are unnecessarily restrictive and fail to grasp fiction as a
heuristic device that can redescribe reality. The question of
meaning in poetry raises the issue of its relation to ideology,
and we will explore the current critical debate on that relationship. We will then analyze how reference may be achieved in
metaphorical discourse and draw some implications for our
reading of poetry.

I

Before we consider how reference is achieved despite poetry's
being fictional, we should see what can occur—and to a great

63

extent has occurred—in separating the aesthetic impact of poetic structure from the referential content of the poem's language. Seminal in this development has been Roman Jakobson's definition of the poetic function of language as "the focus
on the message for its own sake."[2] As Jonathan Culler points
out: "By 'message' Jakobson does not, of course, mean 'proposi-
tional content' (that is stressed by the referential function of
language) but simply the utterance itself as a linguistic form. In
Mukarovsky's words, 'the function of poetic language consists
in the maximum foregrounding of the utterance.' "[3] Such critics
limit the aesthetic convention in literature to the linguistic
structure alone. Michael Riffaterre, for instance, writes, "literature can be defined as a linguistic phenomenon in which form
is more important than content, and . . . this phenomenon is
above all a playing with words."[4] Such a poetics in its logical
extreme denies one dimension of language by using it without
reference, perhaps without sense, simply as patterns of acoustic
images and signs. Without reference, poetry becomes little
more than a play of signifiers for sophisticated entertainment—
at its extreme, merely corporeal writing. Criticizing Jakobson
precisely for seeming to declare any linguistic pattern poetic,
Culler insists that the pattern must have a semantic function in
the poem as a communication: "one has an instance of the
poetic function only when one can point to effects which might
be explained as the result of particular projections of the principle of equivalence into the axis of combination."[5] An un-
bridgeable gap between the signifier and signified finally turns
structure into content, as Frederic Jameson observes: "literary
works are about language, take the process of speech or writing
itself as their essential subject matter."[6]

An attempt to separate the structural from the referential
qualities in poetry can easily lead to valuing only the abstrac-
tions of proportion and pattern. Such a view makes poetry into
a sunset, a free rather than a dependent beauty, in Kant's
terms. Drawing on, importantly, Kant himself, Hans-Georg
Gadamer insists we must look beyond the purity of an aesthetics of free beauty to do justice to art: "Kant's demonstration
that the beautiful pleases without a concept does not gainsay
the fact that [also according to Kant] only the beautiful thing
that seems significant to us evokes our total interest. The very
recognition of the non-conceptuality of taste leads beyond an
aesthetic of mere taste."[7] Form for the sake of form leads to an

"aesthetic uncommittedness" which, as Kierkegaard understood, tends to make a religion of aesthetic values.

II

We need not treat poetry in either/or terms—either structural
or referential content. Peter Brooks's point should be well
taken: "One can at the same time accept Culler's argument for
a reading grounded in poetics, and think that the difficult question of the movement 'from word to world' very much needs
attention."[8] The poetic text can, in redescribing reality, function
as a discourse. Critics like Riffaterre, however, refuse to acknowledge any referential function in poetry to what in ordinary usage is called reality or the actual. Even Roman Ingarden
seems willing to assert only the aesthetic worth of the congruity
between structure and idea, though he does claim that the aesthetic experience has a direct relationship to the "quality of
life": the reader's "apprehend[ing] the congruity between the
metaphysical quality and the essential configuration of the situation [gives] an extraordinary sense of life and thereby also a
moment of . . . exceptional conjunction."[9] Gadamer insists more
directly on the movement "from word to world": "even the
phenomenon of art imposes a task on existence; namely . . .
achieving that continuity of self-understanding which alone can
support human existence. . . . The experience of art must not
be side-tracked into the uncommittedness of the aesthetic
awareness. This negative insight, expressed positively, means
that art is knowledge and the experience of the work of art is a
sharing of this knowledge."[10]
   Marxist critics generally, including the *Tel Quel* group of
critics who have worked from principles of poststructuralism,
have also insisted that literary art is more than simply an aesthetic structure.[11] Their concerns, however, have focused on the
relation of literature's referential and structural contents to
ideology. The question has been, not whether literature has
meaning, but how that meaning is produced—as reflection or
transformation of ideology. The "transformationists" have produced a substantial body of critical theory and practice, analyzing how specific literary techniques and forms achieved this
transformation or distancing of ideology. "According to both
the Formalists and the Altusserians," says Tony Bennett in *Formalism and Marxism,* "the literary text affords a triple structure

of vision. First, it offers a vision of the habituated forms on which it works, casting them in a new light by virtue of the transformation to which it subjects them. Second, and in so doing, the literary text prises 'reality' away from the terms of reference which normally condition our access to the social world and thus produces a perception of unexpected aspects of that world. Finally, the literary text offers a vision of its own formal operations, revealing itself as the product of a transformation in the disjunction or tension between the two levels—the 'literary' and the 'ideological'—which account for its real complexity."[12] These Formalists and Altusserians hold that literature offers special access to what is "real."

More recently, the question has become, not whether literary forms distance ideology, but whether the revealing contradictions are inherent in language itself as it is used by different social classes. "Far from seeing literary practice as an activity which makes visible the operations of dominant ideology in any transparent sense, it is now argued [by such critics as Renée Balibar and Dominique Laporte] that literary practice constitutes an essentially ideological operation in its attempts to heal or placate class and ideological contradictions inscribed within language itself."[13] Bennett repeatedly objects to what he calls the "essentializing" of literature as a category: "The formulation that literary texts work on and transform dominant ideological forms so as to 'reveal' or 'distance' them . . . is impossible to sustain. It is rather Marxist criticism which, through an active and critical intervention, so 'works' upon the texts concerned as to make them 'reveal' or 'distance' the dominant ideological forms to which they are made to 'allude.' "[14] Rather than their analyzing how literature through its devices is able to distance ideology, these critics now assume that the language used as raw material in literature is the language of ideology and that the contradictions within ideology can be revealed only by a conscious effort in production—conscious by the critic, if not by the author.

The question now has become whether the text has any meaning that counts. Drawing on Pierre Macherey's concept of the text's "unconscious," believing that "the task of criticism . . . is to establish the unspoken in the text, to decentre it in order to produce a real knowledge of history,"[15] Catherine Belsey calls for a "productive" or "scientific" criticism, which "recognizes in the text no 'knowledge' but ideology itself in all its inconsistency and partiality."[16] Because ideology "obscures the real conditions of existence by presenting partial truths"[17] and because the raw material of the text is the language of ideology, "the object of the critic . . . is to seek not the unity of the work, but the multiplicity and diversity of its possible meanings, its incompleteness, the omissions which it displays but cannot describe, and above all its contradictions. In its absences, and in the collisions between its divergent meanings, the text implicitly criticizes its own ideology."[18] Arguing that all criticism is political, that the category "literature" may be a useless formulation, that those critical works which focus on the text as artful communication unconsciously support the bourgeois ideology, many contemporary Marxist critics are deconstructing "the metaphysics of the text" and insisting on "the Death of the Author"—"the liberation of the text from the authority of a presence behind it which gives it meaning. Released from the constraints of a single and univocal reading, the text becomes available for production, plural, contradictory, capable of change."[19] Theorists calling for productive criticism seem not to accept that literature should be considered an artful communication to be fully understood on its own terms before being utilized in some different discourse.

An important exception is Jameson, who, in *The Political Unconscious,* cautions against reifying the social ground (as well as the structure) and thus *losing the text as such:*

> to insist on either of the two inseparable yet incommensurable dimensions of the symbolic act without the other: to overemphasize the active way in which the text reorganizes its subtext (in order, presumably, to reach the triumphant conclusion that the 'referent' does not exist); or on the other hand to stress the imaginary status of the symbolic act so completely as to reify its social ground, now no longer understood as a subtext but merely as some inert given that the text passively or fantasmatically 'reflects'—to overstress either of these functions of the symbolic act at the expense of the other is surely to produce sheer ideology, whether it be, as in the first alternative, the ideology of structuralism, or, in the second, that of vulgar materialism.[20]

Jameson, following Paul Ricoeur, concludes that the unmasking of ideology masquerading as truth is a negative hermeneutics, suggesting that a positive hermeneutics is needed as well—though his discussion of one focuses on a hermeneutics of culture.[21] For our study, we will take up that positive hermeneutics of the metaphorical text to see how the text itself establishes reference and thus makes a statement about what is—or what seems to be, which is all we can assert. We will then see the role negative hermeneutics (or, to use Ricoeur's terms, a hermeneutics of suspicion) has to play in a positive hermeneutics (hermeneutics of beliefs).

III

Even without the insights of post-Saussurean linguistics, the relation between poetry and knowledge would now be seen as more complex than had generally been acknowledged before Marx, Nietzsche, and Freud—more complex but still intact. Gadamer's assertion that art offers knowledge immediately raises the perennial question: how can the fictional have any meaning that can count as knowledge if knowledge is defined (positivistically) as propositions that are certain? Indeed, a current skeptical view is that all so-called knowledge is fictional, because it is inevitably an imaginative construct, an interpretation, and therefore not at all certain. Significantly, Altusser's concept of ideology "as *the necessary condition* of action within the social formation"[22] has profound implications for eliminating dogmatisms in knowledge.[23] Marxists, as well as everyone else, have—and must have—ideologies: "Because ideology has the role of constituting concrete individuals as subjects, because it is produced in the identification with the 'I' of discourse, and is thus the condition of action, we cannot simply step outside it. To do so would be to refuse to act or speak, and even to make such a refusal, to say 'I refuse,' is to accept the condition of subjectivity."[24] No experience is unmediated by either language or ideology, but to accept our essential subjectivity is not to lose all possibility of objectivity, some means of getting beyond our own perspectives and some means of testing the reliability of what we think we know.

We may acknowledge the infinite regress of absolute knowledge without being forced into the absurd position of abandoning the concepts of knowledge and truth. As Nicholas Rescher cogently argues in *Methodological Pragmatism,* if one is to engage at all in the cognitive enterprise, one must accept defensible procedures for inquiry which in turn produce knowledge as legitimate and "certain" in a reasonable sense.[25] Marxist critiques of bourgeois ideology, Freud's "discovery" of the unconscious, the current deconstructions of our constructs—all serve to expose contradictions in our knowledge we are then called on to resolve discursively in a process of continually achieving the best information and understanding possible. Its not being absolute should preclude our being dogmatic; its being the most reliable we have gives us a reasonable basis on which to act.

If the principles and methods are defensible, relativity in knowledge contrasts, not with objectivity, but with *absoluteness.* Furthermore, the philosophical shifts from objective reason to subjective reason to intersubjective reason have illustrated that we can attack the current reasoning only by means of a new and broader definition of reason. For instance, all the current "decoding" analyses in criticism presuppose that deconstructionist principles and methods can produce knowledge, verifiable statements about what is. Indeed, the assumption seems to be that their making visible the invisible forces that determine our attitudes and actions can liberate us from being unconsciously controlled. It is this greater knowledge, our understanding something more than we did before, from which the deconstructionists derive the stance and tone of authority even while they are questioning authority itself.

In language, however, the gap between the signifier and the signified, if pushed to the extreme of uncertainty, calls into question not only an Absolute but even reference itself. Language is blind, and literature is opaque. Poetry may be valued precisely because it seems not to claim knowledge. Meaning in poetry, however, is neither to be privileged nor dismissed because it is not absolute nor even systematic. Poetry is a different form of discourse, showing truth in Heidegger's sense of disclosedness, insight. In an impressive analysis in *Languages of Art* Nelson Goodman demonstrates that artistic representation is one form of denotation; thus whatever is represented with aesthetic excellence will entail cognitive excellence. In supporting a denotative theory of art, Goodman distinguishes between description and representation but shows both to be categories of reference.[26] Similarly, George Lakoff and Mark Johnson, in *Metaphors We Live By,* show how metaphorical thinking is basic to our conceptual system and can be best described as "imaginative rationality."[27] In contrast, Justus Buchler, a contemporary philosopher who analyzes meaning in art, distinguishes three modes of judgment—assertive or rational, exhibitive or artistic, and active or moral—all of which communicate meaning, but only assertive judgment makes a truth-claim.[28] My disagreement with Buchler's position will be discussed after considering Ricoeur's insights in the next section.

IV

Can words in poetry have reference not only beyond that fateful gap between signifier and signified but also beyond the fictional to the actual, insofar as we can have reasonable certainty about what is? Culler rightly points out that our making sense of metaphors in a positive hermeneutic presupposes our expectations of unity and referentiality of texts: "The question of metaphor arises only where there is a problem in the text, a perception of incongruity. And therefore in the first instance the notion of metaphor depends on a series of models of *vraisemblance* and coherence which allow us to perceive a statement as incongruous or incoherent. . . . This conclusion depends in turn on conventions about the unity and referentiality of literary works."[29] To a greater extent than any other theorist, Paul Ricoeur analyzes in detail how the metaphorical expression establishes reference to the actual and makes a statement about what is. Metaphor, he shows, has two levels of reference ("split reference") within its context: "it both is and it is not."[30] For instance, consider the opening metaphor in Frost's "November":

> We saw leaves go to glory,
> Then almost migratory
> Go half way down the lane,
> And then to end the story
> Get beaten down and pasted
> In one wild day of rain.
> We heard " 'Tis over" roaring.
> A year of leaves was wasted.
> Oh, we make a boast of storing,
> Of saving and of keeping,
> But only by ignoring
> The waste of moments sleeping,
> The waste of pleasure weeping,
> By denying and ignoring
> The waste of nations warring.

The first line is metaphorical, illustrating the split reference: literally, the leaves do not "go to glory," a phrase which makes "glory" a place to which one can travel. (The now dated meaning of the phrase is, of course, to go to heaven.) The archaic flavor of this phrase minimizes the "is not" dimension of the split reference in metaphor. Such a depreciation of the "is not" dimension is a characteristic of many of Frost's metaphors, which will have a current, common usage, minimizing the "semantic impertinence" while that "impertinence" is still sufficiently there for the very subtle word plays that Frost loves. Frost's weighting the "is" side of the split reference is partly why his poems have a realistic tone, and here "go to glory" suggests directly, almost literally, the splendor and brilliance of fall colors. Still, the reference is split, and for Frost—and us—all the fun is in the "as-if."

The fun in the split reference is also how the new meaning is achieved: through the insertion of the heuristic device of fiction—the "is not" dimension of the metaphor—metaphor redescribes reality. Ricoeur explains: "It is within the very analysis of the metaphorical statement that a referential conception of poetic language must be established, a conception that takes account of the elimination of the [first] reference. . . . Within the perspective of semantic impertinence, the self-destruction of meaning is merely the other side of *an innovation in meaning* that constitutes living metaphors."[31] This new semantic pertinence, which "cannot take place without fusion, without intuitive passage," Ricoeur calls a "seeing-as." As a distinguishing characteristic of metaphorical discourse, this intuited "seeing-as" links a verbal and nonverbal moment in an "experience-act" which is the "sensible" or "iconic" moment of metaphor, drawn from the concreteness presented in the first-level reference.[32] It is in the "seeing-as" moment in metaphor that we intuit a redescription of reality, and that redescription is an assertion, a metaphorical truth, a statement about what is.

In this theory what happens at the level of a metaphorical sentence can also happen at the level of the text; the second-level reference establishes a "world" of the text—imaginatively, a way of being to which we can relate our actual ways of being. In "November," for instance, we intuit the profoundly disturbing futility and waste of the human suffering in wars through a metaphoric "seeing-as" which relates the loss of a crop of autumn leaves (and the progressively more disturbing "wastes" in sleeping, then weeping) to the futility of wars. The redescription of reality that is achieved, in the context of the understatement, is the horrifying waste in wars of what humans value. This intuited perception is no less than an assertion about what is, insofar as we can know it.

As metaphor creates the resemblance (rather than finding and expressing it), we "discover," and the logic or acceptability of what we discover—the redescription—is tested against our experience and also against such deconstructions as the critique of ideologies, our awareness of the manifestations of the unconscious, and so forth. Metaphorical truth has dimensions of correspondence and coherence in our worlds, though the justification for the intuited judgment is the result, not of argumentative discourse, but of the logic of discovery: "it must be new but fitting, strange but evident, surprising but satisfying. A simple labeling does not equal a 're-sorting'; new discriminations, new organization must result from the emigration of a schema."[33] The logic of discovery draws on both analysis and synthesis, explanation and understanding.

Buchler's defining artistic meaning as the exhibitive or structural arrangement[34] is too limited for metaphor, in which an assertion occurs in the "experience-act" of "seeing-as." Buchler's emphasis is appropriate to the extent that this metaphorical assertion is not supported by explicit argumentation but is instead the result of the exhibitive dimension, the juxtaposition of the two categories. However, metaphor cannot be understood simply in its exhibitive meaning; with the logic of discovery, the intuition from that juxtaposition may be an assertion. Thus it is that the second-level reference opens out, beyond our experience of the poem's unity and autonomy, into our worlds through its redescription of reality.

The analysis in negative hermeneutics, it should be noted, also requires the reader's intuited passage and also redescribes reality, but in the sense of deconstructing, or reducing our illusions. As we have seen Jameson suggest, the various negative hermeneutics are not adequate in themselves for our determining positive meaning, interpretations of reality to which persons can subscribe. The role of negative hermeneutics within the scope of positive hermeneutics, as Ricoeur elaborates in *Hermeneutics and the Human Sciences,* constitutes a part of the explanatory or objective phases of interpretation. With structuralism, linguistics, and other such "sciences," negative hermeneutics help establish the *sense* of the text; the intuited passage of the second-level reference establishes the "world" of the text with its potential for increasing our understanding through its redescription of reality. The explanatory phases of interpretation should not be considered ends in themselves but should *lead to* the reader's understanding of the world of text—that is, finally to the reader's appropriation of the text. So that the text is not lost in the process of interpretation, readers should not merely subjectively impose themselves on the text; in appropriating the text, they enlarge their own horizons by understanding the world of text in relation to themselves.[35] That understanding, of course, may lead them to reject that redescription of reality as significant for themselves; not all redescriptions are insightful, but the point is they may be.

Valuing only the text's "unconscious" or valuing only structure in poetry eliminates the intuited discoveries from metaphoric redescriptions. Structure can order chaos but not permanently so as to eliminate chaos from life: the imagination can accommodate tragedy but cannot change it. Indeed, Frost is so much aware how much of life is left out of a poetics which values form for itself that his poetry often points up the contrast between the carefully structured, controlled form and the open-ended content that reveals how much of life the human being cannot control after all. Recognizing those limits led Robert Frost to see the poem as "the constant symbol of the figure of the will braving alien entanglements" and as "a momentary stay against confusion."[36] In "November," for instance, both nature and human nature defy any final transformation from the poem's shaping force, while the poem's form creates a powerful effect of controlled structure. By means of the intoxicatingly tight patterns, the poem almost overcomes the final horror of "the waste of nations warring." However, the ironic force is that, while the poem evokes a sense of strong pattern, the referential content bursts the bounds of that sense of control. The strong rhythm, feminine rhyme, frequency of repeated sounds in trimeter couplets, all convey clearly discernible patterns. Moreover, the poet carefully creates a sense of the continuousness of such actions by the repetition of gerunds. We have the sense that the experience has been strongly shaped, which effect then makes even sharper and more shocking the contrast between the poet's control in the structure and the human inability to control events as described in the referential content. Indeed, much modern poetry turns on this same ironic contrast.

The totality of the poem, then, is more than its structural content or its referential content; the totality is the interaction which we intuit. We can see that, while structure is not simply transparent in poetry, poetic structure need not be so opaque that it constitutes the total effect, as Jakobson and others assume. Indeed, to the extent that literature has referential content, Mary Louise Pratt's argument is well taken that "literary" structures are basically the same as those of all speech acts and cannot in themselves be the definitive characteristics of literature.[37]

V

But there is a crucial distinction between metaphorical discourse and utilitarian prose: in the latter the reader does not have to construct a second-level reference whereas the poem "affords us the opportunity of intuiting its idea [through the aesthetic surface,] through the congruity of the work's aesthetic qualities."[38] Because poetry is both aesthetic and fictional, it is not only autonomous—a self-enclosed unity that achieves a finalization—but heteronomous as well: it requires the reader's imaginative participation not only to fill in the gaps in its first-level reference but also to effect the "intuited passage" to its second-level reference. Poetry is essentially language structured to evoke reader-participation and particularly to evoke a range of experiential and intellectual responses. As readers of poetry, we engage the poem's immediacy, sensuousness, dramatization, iconicity, and indeterminacy—all dimensions of experience more than dimensions of abstracted information, all involving imaginative response necessary to intuitions of the poem's second-level reference. Edward Casey calls these intuited second-level references "insights":

> Art suggests by evoking; in this way, it does not operate in an implicit or tacit manner. . . . Paradoxically, [art] gives us this insight [into reality] by keeping our attention riveted onto the aesthetic surface, where primary meanings are among the first objects of our regard. We are led to insight when a primary meaning gestures expressively toward a secondary meaning. This means that artistic truth, the object of aesthetic insight, cannot be expressed adequately in any form or medium other than the precise one in which it is concretely presented.[39]

In just this way, Bakhtin's detailed critique of formalism turns on a form-content fusion, "a chemical combination,"[40] as the source of what he calls the finalization of any literary text.

Precisely because poetry is structured so that the reader participates in constructing as well as responding to both the structural and referential content, we have a dual awareness in our experience of poetry: we are aware of its being poetry (aesthetic and fictional) while we are also experiencing its internal perspective. Perhaps the most obvious example of our having both perspectives occurs when we are watching a play: although we are identifying with, say, Hamlet, we do not rush up on to the stage to save Hamlet when the fight scene is staged. The willing suspension of disbelief goes only so far. Rather than our attention being focused more narrowly in our experience of a poem, our attention is actually increased: because the poetic structures have semantic functions, we attend to the appropriateness of both what is represented as well as how it is represented. We are responding more than usual, not only to reference, but also to what can be called the poem's iconicity. A current emphasis in critical reading, particularly in deconstruction, makes the reader's response to the text not only highly conscious but also thoroughly analytical. Nonetheless, the reader also participates by intuiting, identifying—initially, in making sense of the text, and finally, in appropriating the text to enlarge his own horizons.

We can also conclude that a part of poetry's particular forcefulness is that its structures as well as its references have persuasive effect. In the terms of speech-act theory, this particular power in poetry comes from the performance clues being to a great extent our own; the meanings are created in our "intuited passage" to the second-level reference; we simply believe our own experience, as it were. Significantly, because literature stimulates these imaginative responses, we intuit, as our own deep experiences, other perspectives besides our own. Through an imaginative leap into the world of the speaker's perspective, we can experience, at least in part, how that world seems from within. This participation in others' perspectives is a particular effect of the "experience-act" of "seeing-as," intuiting an assertive meaning through the concreteness of an exhibitive meaning rather than understanding the assertion in abstracted, rational discourse.

For the reader of the poetry this dual awareness of aesthetic distance and imaginative identification means that the poem's language is both looked at and looked through. To minimize either the structural or the referential content is to lose no less than poetic truth as discovery.

Notes

1. Siegfried J. Schmidt, *Foundation for the Empirical Study of Literature,* trans. Robert de Beaugrande (Hamburg: Helmut Buske, 1982), pp. 74–109. What I term *fiction* is herein elaborated from the characteristic of polyvalence—a word's having several meanings—in literature. I am using *meaning* in this paper in its general denotation as "the idea conveyed to the mind." Webster's *Seventh New Collegiate Dictionary* designates *meaning* as "the general term used of anything (as a word, sign, poem, or action) requiring or allowing of interpretation." I use *sense,* as do linguists, to distinguish the signified from the referent of a word.

2. Roman Jakobson, "Linguistics and Poetics," in *Style in Language,* ed. T. Sebeok (Cambridge, Mass.: M.I.T. Press, 1960), p. 354.

3. Jonathan Culler, *Structuralist Poetics* (Ithaca, N.Y.: Cornell University Press, 1975), p. 56.

4. Michael Riffaterre, *Semiotics of Poetry* (Bloomington, Ind.: Indiana University Press, 1978), p. 125.

5. Culler, *Structuralist Poetics,* p. 66.

6. Frederic Jameson, *The Prison-House of Language: A Critical Account of Structuralism and Russian Formalism* (Princeton, N.J.: Princeton University Press, 1972), p. 199.

7. Hans-Georg Gadamer, *Truth and Method* (New York: Crossroad Pub. Co., 1982) p. 46.

8. Peter Brooks, "Fiction and Its Referents: A Reappraisal, *Poetics Today* 4 (Spring 1983): 74.

9. Eugene H. Falk, *The Poetics of Roman Ingarden* (Chapel Hill, N.C.: University of North Carolina Press, 1981), p. 19.

10. Gadamer, *Truth and Method,* p. 87.

11. Frederic Jameson's emphasis on the significance of literary form for Marxist criticism in *Marxism and Form* (Princeton, N.J.: Princeton University Press, 1971) provided impetus for analyses of structural contents that had not previously been a major concern for Marxist critics.

12. Tony Bennett, *Formalism and Marxism* (London: Methuen, 1979), p. 129.

13. Ibid., p. 161.

14. Ibid., p. 141.

15. Catherine Belsey, *Critical Practice* (London: Methuen, 1980), p. 136.

16. Ibid., p. 128.

17. Ibid., p. 57.

18. Ibid., p. 109.

19. Ibid., p. 134.

20. Frederic Jameson, *The Political Unconscious: Narrative as a Socially Symbolic Act* (Ithaca, N.Y.: Cornell University Press, 1981), p. 82.

21. See Jameson, *The Political Unconscious,* chap. 6, "Conclusion: The Dialectic of Utopia and Ideology," pp. 281–99.

22. Belscy, *Critical Practice*, p. 57; emphasis mine.

23. Both Bennett and Belsey acknowledge these implications. See *Formalism and Marxism*, pp. 137–42, and *Critical Practice*, pp. 62–65.

24. Belsey, *Critical Practice*, p. 62.

25. Nicholas Rescher, *Methodological Pragmatism: A Systems-Theoretic Approach to the Theory of Knowledge* (Oxford: Basil Blackwell, 1977) esp. pp. 201–34.

26. Nelson Goodman, *Languages of Art: An Approach to a Theory of Symbols* (New York: Bobbs-Merrill, 1968). See especially chap. 6, "Art and the Understanding."

27. George Lakoff and Mark Johnson, *Metaphors We Live By* (Chicago: University of Chicago Press, 1977), p. 235.

28. Justus Buchler, *Toward a General Theory of Human Judgment* (New York: Columbia University Press, 1951).

29. Jonathan Culler, "Commentary" in the issue On Metaphor, *New Literary History* 6 (Autumn 1974): 225.

30. Paul Ricoeur, *The Rule of Metaphor: Multi-disciplinary Studies of the Creation of Meaning in Language,* trans. Robert Czerny with Kathleen McLaughlin and John Costello, SJ (Toronto: University of Toronto Press, 1977), p. 224.

31. Ricoeur, *The Rule of Metaphor,* p. 230; emphasis mine.

32. Ibid., pp. 212–15.

33. Ibid., p. 237.

34. Justus Buchler, *The Main of Light* (New York: Oxford University Press, 1974).

35. Paul Ricoeur, *Hermeneutics and the Human Sciences: Essays on Language, Action and Interpretation,* trans. and ed. John B. Williams (Cambridge: Cambridge University Press, 1981). See especially the following essays: "The Hermeneutical Function of Distanciation," "What Is a Text? Explanation and Understanding," and "Appropriation."

36. Hyde Cox and Edward Connery Lathem, eds., *Selected Prose of Robert Frost* (New York: Holt, Rinehart and Winston, 1966), pp. 18, 25.

37. Mary Louise Pratt, *Toward a Speech Act Theory of Literary Discourse* (Bloomington, Ind.: Indiana University Press, 1977).

38. Falk, *Poetics of Roman Ingarden*, p. 149.

39. Edward S. Casey, "Truth in Art," *Man and World* 3 (1970): 363.

40. M. M. Bahktin and P. N. Medvedev, *The Formal Method in Literary Scholarship: A Critical Introduction to Sociological Poetics,* trans. Albert J. Werle (Baltimore, Md.: Johns Hopkins University Press, 1978), p. 140.

Text and
Interpretation

The Unaccommodating Text: The Critical Situation of *Timon of Athens*

Thomas Cartelli

Muhlenberg College

I

T HE "corrupt text on the subject of absolute corruption" that is *Timon of Athens* has attracted a disproportionately small number of sympathetic scholars to the task of making dramatic sense of the play's own disproportionate blend of "icy precepts" and "sweet degrees."[1] The text's very corruption has, moreover, provoked even some of the play's most fervent supporters to attempt the critical transformation of this obviously unpolished play into an image and likeness that accords with prevailing standards of Shakespearean dramatic integrity and decorum.[2] It has also led others, equally sympathetic but more interested in what the play itself has to say, to explore the underpinnings and most crucial motivations of Shakespeare's approach to his dramatic art.[3] But probably the most common tendency of recent Shakespeare criticism has been simply to dismiss the play from sustained consideration, not on the basis of its textual corruption, but on account of its apparent single-mindedness, its unaccommodating commitment to its protagonist's stubbornly inflexible point of view. Norman Rabkin formulates his own version of this critical position in the following terms:

> The trouble with *Timon of Athens* is that it is not complementary. . . .
> at no point do we encounter such tensions as Shakespearean
> tragedy has elsewhere involved us in. . . . Because Shakespeare
> seems to assume a simple moral position, the play is uniquely un-
> able to call into question the nature of being. It never seems . . . to
> get down to the unresolvable conflicts with which . . . *King Lear,*
> *Coriolanus, Antony and Cleopatra,* and *Othello* are primarily con-
> cerned.[4]

Rabkin articulates this position with his usual judiciousness and
precision; he describes in a very straightforward manner the
problem many of us have had in attempting to reconcile *Timon*
with plays that hold both the mind and the stage with greater
power and authority. But in basing his own dismissal of *Timon*
on its lack of complementarity (an arguable proposition in its
own right), Rabkin localizes the "trouble" with *Timon* in the
context of the play's failure to provide what the critic is looking
for and has come to expect, and thus transfers to the play what
may well be the trouble with his critical ideology.[5] Since *Timon*
does not seem to generate "unresolvable conflicts" of the variety associated with more canonically respectable texts, the
conflicts that the play does generate are ignored and the play
itself is effectively excluded from critical discourse. In the process, the play is implicitly assigned the status of an unaccommodating text, that is, a text that is inconsistent with the prevailing critical consensus concerning what a Shakespearean
tragedy is or should be, does or should do. Rabkin's privileging
of complementarity thus serves the combined purpose of pre-
serving a canonical distinction and a critical predisposition at
the expense of sacrificing a potentially provocative critical encounter with a text that may call into question the whole process
by which such judgments were arrived at in the first place.
　　In taking issue with *Timon*'s critical reputation in this manner,
I do not mean to suggest that *Timon* is not as single-minded a
play or as unaccommodating a text as Rabkin implies; nor do I
mean to set into motion a process that will raise *Timon*'s value in
the critical marketplace or in the Shakespearean canon. Rather,
I mean to clear interpretive ground for readings of *Timon* that
are more consistent with the play's peculiar dramatic aims and
organization than most past readings have been, and to do so in
a manner that is less committed to a critical idiom and ideology
alien to the peculiar nature of dramatic texts. It seems to me
that what finally distinguishes *Timon* from Shakespeare's other

tragedies is not its failure but its refusal to be complementary in the way Rabkin describes. In *Timon* Shakespeare appears deliberately to refuse to accommodate the disruptions of tragic experience to the consolations effected by dramatic strategies that seek to redeem or, at least, moderate the expression of waste or loss. This refusal is combined in the play with an equally bold attempt on Shakespeare's part to have his audience assume an unusually active role in monitoring and evaluating its own responses to the play's protagonist, who similarly refuses to accommodate himself to conventional expectations but who has no sustained rival in his claim on audience sympathy and attention. The unaccommodating text of the drama becomes in this fashion the occasion for a radical experiment in the psychology of theatrical experience, an experiment that requires its audience both to identify and to engage in a critical dialogue with a character who is at once its bane and its ideal, its representative and its accuser, the anatomizer and embodiment of its own values and assumptions.[6] This experiment is radical to the extent that it remains faithful to the dramatic logic of its own conclusions, denying Timon as it denies its audience recourse to strategies that might serve to redeem, resolve, or otherwise reduce the prevailing pressure of bitterness and rage that firmly establishes itself at the close of the play's third act and maintains its hold on the drama through to the end.

It is, of course, *Timon*'s unswerving devotion to its chosen dramatic idiom that is responsible for its historic failure to command an "understanding auditory" fully sympathetic to what has often been construed as a denial of art itself. As Susan Handelman states in one of the more penetrating recent appraisals of the play:

> In *Timon of Athens* disillusion is absolute, no substitute is acceptable, there are no rituals of atonement, no provisions for mourning. The play is less about the experience of loss itself than a demonstration of the rage which refuses to accept loss. Perhaps this is why it is generally considered to be a bad play—it does not do what we expect of art in general: help us to accept loss.[7]

In making her point, Handelman seems to assign primary responsibility for *Timon*'s failure to find its audience to the play itself, particularly to the play's refusal to accommodate itself to its audience's psychological needs and aesthetic expectations. But her statement also implies that *Timon*'s refusal to "help us to accept loss" is reciprocated by our own refusal to meet the unusual challenges posed by a play that upsets our conventional notions about the uses of art. Although Handelman, herself, might object to the uses to which I am putting her argument, I find her providing here a rather crucial insight into the critical tendency to deny or dismiss works of art that define themselves in terms of refusal or rejection, instead of conforming to an aesthetic of accommodation or compromise upon which we have come too often to rely.[8] In refusing to provide us with "rituals of atonement" consistent with this aesthetic, *Timon* is effectively calling the aesthetic itself into question, is attempting to extend the range of tragic expression beyond the pale of dramatic proprieties that serve to defend or protect us from unmediated involvement in tragic experience. In so doing, *Timon* may, admittedly, be demanding more of us than we are normally accustomed to give in relation to theatrical productions; it may be requiring us to break critical habits of mind that are ineluctably tied to our psychological need for defenses against precisely the kinds of denial with which *Timon* is preoccupied.

It is the possibility that such habits of mind can, indeed, be broken (especially at a time when so many of us are actively involved in the demystification of critical and cultural assumptions) that I intend to entertain in the following in order to provide *Timon* with the new reading I believe it deserves: a reading premised on the notion that in *Timon* Shakespeare is consciously engaged in revising his own aesthetic in an effort to bring "unaccommodated man" into the affective orbit of an auditory held captive by its very presence in the theater. Such a notion clearly suggests an insight into Shakespeare's intentions for his play that no one can claim with assurance. I make provisional claim to such insight here in order to give Shakespeare's facility as a playwright priority in discussing the play's dramatic effects, and also to counter the tendency to see in the playtext's corruption evidence of a compositional breakdown, the formal remains of an unresolved conflict between Shakespeare's actual or original intentions and the intractable matter he had taken for his subject. Of this theory's proponents, Handelman makes the most persuasive case:

All the questions about [*Timon's*] authorship, which stem from the many confusions and disjunctions in the text, indicate an unfinished play which somewhere broke down, would not allow itself to be composed. But that indeed . . . is itself what the play is about—a breakdown of all those ways in which rage, pain, and loss can somehow be accepted, made sense of, transformed into life-affirming energies.[9]

Handelman again seems perfectly correct in respect to "what the play is about," but when she connects the play's dramatic breakdowns with a sympathetic breakdown in the compositional process itself, she tends to make Shakespeare more the victim than the master of his own intentions and to define the play in terms of the same rhetoric of accommodation that gave us *Timon*'s lack of complementarity.[10] Shakespeare does, of course, go to some trouble in the text of the play as we have it to mediate our generally inescapable involvement with Timon; the Alcibiades subplot, the "normative" incursions of Flavius, as well as the sometimes nagging monomania of Timon himself, all seem to constitute gestures in this direction. But each also seems sufficiently half-hearted and ambiguous to suggest that Shakespeare did not intend his audience to escape so easily from the disturbing implications of Timon's extreme position, which is, in the end, more a culmination of than a divergence from Shakespeare's recent preoccupation with the tragic predicament and with the dramatic forms required to express it. It may, therefore, be more reasonable to assume that compositional strategies which permitted Shakespeare to provide at least the outlines of reconciliation in the great tragedies either proved insufficient in relation to *Timon*, or—an alternative I find more convincing—simply inappropriate to the kind of play Shakespeare was writing. The inefficacy of such strategies in *Timon*, rather than serving as evidence of Shakespeare's inability to achieve his intentions, may, in short, help us better to understand just what his intentions were.[11]

Richard Fly approaches the problem of intentionality with a more obvious regard for Shakespeare's control over his own experiment, but, like Handelman, ultimately identifies the process of accommodation as a basic component of the tragic medium itself:

> In his monomaniac actions and language Timon has been slowly destroying himself as a dramatic entity by attacking the very structure that sustains his being. Shakespeare's apparent willingness to attend the misanthrope on his drift towards non-being suggests his own temporary commitment to a concomitant aesthetic suicide. He

appears to have designed a play licensed to pursue its own generic collapse by a perverse rejection of its own medium.[12]

What is especially noteworthy about Fly's formulation is his explicit identification of Timon's rejection of the world's values with Shakespeare's rejection of his own aesthetic standards, his designation as "perverse" Shakespeare's refusal to provide either his play or his audience with what Fly terms a "middle ground of compromise and moderation."[13] The question Fly provokes here is whether "Shakespeare's apparent willingness to attend" Timon so unconditionally really must issue in "a concomitant aesthetic suicide," in "a play licensed to pursue its own generic collapse," as opposed to encouraging the collapse and consequent revision of our own critical categories. Fly avoids having to dwell on the consequences of his own formulation by critically disengaging Shakespeare from Timon in his discussion of the closing movement of the play where he contends that "Timon succumbs to suicidal silence, but Shakespeare goes on to finish the play in a new key" by returning "to the abandoned world of mediation, the carefully excluded 'middle of humanity'" embodied by the now moderate and forgiving Alcibiades.[14] But those of us who are less willing than Fly to accept the seeming even-handedness of a character whom Kenneth Burke has aptly termed a "winsome rotter," and, hence, are less persuaded of the efficacy of what Handelman describes as "an artificial and uncertain resolution" must continue to dwell on the question Fly has answered to his own satisfaction.[15] We must also begin to examine the ways in which a play that so consistently resists accommodating itself to critical rituals of atonement—framed in the idiom of complementarity, compromise, and mediation—may actually be able to explore areas of theatrical experience left unexplored by more obviously balanced dramatic productions.

II

At the end of *King Lear*, Edgar offers a powerful corrective to Albany's understandably human but dramatically inappropriate attempt to compensate for a tragic loss by formalizing his response to it: "The weight of this sad time we must obey, / Speak what we feel, not what we ought to say" (5.3.328–29). Edgar is rejecting here what Nietzsche calls "the mendacious finery" that is the conventional appliance of "the man of culture" in favor of "the unvarnished expression of the truth," which is, in Nietzsche's terms, the true "sphere of poetry."[16] Edgar's corrective resonates throughout the second half of *Timon of Athens*, but nowhere more crucially than in Timon's interview with the Poet and the Painter in 5.1 and in his dialogue with Apemantus in 4.3. In the former scene, Timon responds to the Poet's chronically verbose hypocrisy—"I am rapt, and cannot cover / The monstrous bulk of this ingratitude / With any size of words"—by offering a corrective of his own in regard to the frequently duplicitous relationship that obtains between words and feelings: "Let it go naked, men may see't the better" (5.1.63–66).[17] Without unduly overrating the importance of this one statement in relation to the play as a whole, I would submit that its advocacy of "unvarnished expression" occupies a pivotal role in Shakespeare's attempt to give the unaccommodating spirit of Edgar's remark a more sustained hearing than it could receive within the confines of the earlier play.[18] Letting feelings "go naked" is not, of course, a characteristic procedure of art. Indeed, it can, as Fly suggests, constitute a "rejection" of artistic control that could be construed as "perverse" if in the act of rejection it fails to communicate its purpose to an audience. But there is a second half to Timon's statement that endows his injunction with a positive purpose, and thus makes it appear less a rejection of art than a rejection of the gilded sophistries that pass themselves off as art. The Poet should, according to Timon, let his ingratitude go naked that "men may see't the better," so that it may be made plain and clearly discernible to everyone, hence, impossible to deny. It is here, I believe, that Timon's voice can be confidently identified with that of its author whose evolving aesthetic involves the same uncompromising approach to tragic experience which Timon brings to bear on his succession of personal encounters. That such an approach continues to elicit far more negative critical appraisals than those generated by the similarly disturbing but comparatively more "complementary" *King Lear* may suggest that we are, ourselves, more like the Painter and the Poet than we are like Edgar or Timon. As a consequence of our general uneasiness in regard to feelings that go naked and truths that remain unvarnished, we are likely to be on the lookout, throughout the second half of *Timon*, for other characters with whom we can identify our interests and for

dramatic encounters that will serve either to discredit Timon,
or to place him at a sufficient remove from us so that he might
become the object of our critical scrutiny, instead of our
anatomizer and accuser.

It is just such an area of relief that Shakespeare seems to
provide for us when in 4.3 Apemantus delivers what has ap-
peared to many to be the fatal critical blow against Timon's
uncompromising indictment of the world's corruption:

> The middle of humanity thou never knewest, but
> the extremity of both ends. When thou wast in thy
> gilt and thy perfume, they mock'd thee for too much
> curiosity; in thy rags thou know'st none, but art
> despis'd for the contrary.

$$[4.3.301–5]$$

These are strong and working words. They appeal not only to
our need to reduce Timon to manageable proportions, but to
our prejudice against people who, like Timon, have never had
to endure the perhaps pettier but more perdurable round of
daily defeats and frustration, who, suffering now from a loss of
fortune, never before had a loss to contend with. In short,
Apemantus speaks on behalf of our collective desire to under-
mine the authority of Timon's pronouncements, to invalidate
what he says by invalidating who he is. There is, moreover, a
certain justice in this, especially given the apparent arrogance
and condescension of Timon's immediately prior attempt to
discredit Apemantus: "Thou art a slave, whom Fortune's ten-
der arm / With favour never clasp'd, but bred a dog" (4.3.252–
53). Justice, however, seems meant to occupy but a secondary
role in our response to the extended address of Timon's that
these harsh words initiate. For in the verses that follow, Shakespeare endows Timon's speech with a power, grace, and authority that transcend the ongoing battle of mutual abuse and
recrimination. In so doing, he grants a sudden dignity to the
extreme positions Timon has inhabited, a dignity they will re-
tain even in the face of Apemantus's potent counterattack:[19]

> Hadst thou like us from our first swath proceeded
> The sweet degrees that this brief world affords
> To such as may the passive drugs of it
> Freely command, thou wouldst have plung'd thyself
> In general riot, melted down thy youth
> In different beds of lust, and never learn'd

The icy precepts of respect, but followed
The sugar'd game before thee. But myself—
Who had the world as my confectionary,
The mouths, the tongues, the eyes and hearts of men
At duty, more than I could frame employment:
That numberless upon me stuck, as leaves
Do on the oak, have with one winter's brush
Fell from their boughs and left me open, bare,
For every storm that blows—I, to bear this,
That never knew but better, is some burthen.
Thy nature did commence in sufferance, time
Hath made thee hard in 't. Why shouldst thou hate men?
They never flatter'd thee.

[4.3.254–72]

This speech, providing as it does an influential preface to Apemantus's rejoinder, constitutes a pivotal moment in the play's complex shaping of audience response. The excessive animus toward Apemantus that it betrays both at its beginning and end—"Hence, be gone! / If thou hadst not been born the worst of men, / Thou hadst been a knave and flatterer" (4.3.276–78)—may, as noted above, serve to further alienate an audience that is not sympathetic in the first place to Timon's bias in favor of the prerogatives of privilege. But I believe that the speech is intentionally geared to break down even this audience's resistance to Timon—and to do so *before* Apemantus has an opportunity to respond—by basing its appeal not on a conscious evaluation of what Timon says, but on a more immediate participation in the story he tells.

Shakespeare proceeds here in a manner that is consistent with his ongoing attempt to make his protagonist's approach to the audience both dramatically direct and psychologically provocative, but also in a manner that is uncharacteristic of his writing for Timon in the second half of the play, which is usually phrased in the shrill language of invective. Timon seems meant to surprise us as he recalls with a contagious nostalgia and, in the process, conjures up in remarkably appealing terms the life of pleasure he lived when all the world was his "confectionary." His speech has the effect of awakening in us a shared sympathy for that life (based, perhaps, on our own common fantasies about our respective "golden ages") which tends to disarm us of the censorious attitude we may have previously developed in regard to Timon's earlier prodigality. Clearly, Timon is not "going naked" here in the same way he later suggests the Poet should. But he is going naked in a different and profounder sense by giving us sustained insight into an interior life (inhabited by his own common fantasies) that most critics of the play refuse to believe exists. When Timon speaks of "The mouths, the tongues, the eyes and hearts of men" that once surrounded him with an almost maternal warmth but have now disappeared, he recreates for his audience its own inner narrative of security and separation, compelling it to identify its earliest experience of loss with his present state of abandonment, despite the fact that, on a conscious level, the men of whom Timon speaks were merely servants and suitors "At duty." This largely unconscious (though, perhaps, consciously wrought) bonding between actor and audience is, I would submit, precisely the "stuff" theatrical experience is made upon, a point easy to lose sight of when speeches like this one are read with a profounder regard for surface detail than for the kind of interactional dynamics a playwright must always have in mind. The dynamics of this moment are such that after Timon reaches the peak of his expression of abandonment—in the wonderfully evocative tree/leaves simile—the point he has been moving toward—"I, to bear this," etc.—is made with far greater impact than it could command were we to encounter it in complete isolation from performative considerations. In short, these too are strong and working words and, as such, they make a case for Timon's "extremity of both ends" that no representative of the "middle of humanity" can wholly discredit, especially when the latter must compete against the audience's desire for identification, which generally proves to be a more dominant force than resistance in the peculiar economy of theatrical experience.

Placed in its full performative context, Apemantus's critique of Timon thus loses a great deal of the choric authority that is frequently claimed for it. We may, of course, continue to rely on it as a buffer between ourselves and Timon's more icy precepts, as an endorsement of an ethic of accommodation that opposes itself to Timon's rather subversive claim on our sympathies. But to do so would be at odds with Shakespeare's prevailing approach to such situations throughout the second half of the play, which involves turning our search for areas of relief from Timon into a renewed respect for Timon's rejection of the same. In the present instance, we first expect Apemantus to drive Timon out of his misanthropic humor but actually play witness to a reversal of roles. In an ironic variation on Jonsonian practice, the "fantasist" eventually confutes the "counterfantasist" and disarms him of his presumptive claim to the role of professional demystifier by revealing his own embeddedness in a "middle of humanity" he once professed to disdain.[20] An even more subtle reversal characterizes Timon's encounter with Alcibiades in the first half of 4.3, which, like the ensuing encounter with Apemantus, focuses on a "normative" character with whom an audience might easily identify its interests, but whose own interests come to seem increasingly mercenary. Critics who like to envision Alcibiades as the restorative embodiment of balance and moderation at play's end tend to pass lightly over the company Alcibiades keeps in this scene, and thus fail to make the connection Timon makes in linking the soldier's pursuits with those of his prostitute companions:

> I know thee too, and more than I know thee
> I not desire to know. Follow thy drum;
> With man's blood paint the ground, gules, gules.
> Religious canons, civil laws are cruel;
> Then what should war be? This fell whore of thine
> Hath in her more destruction than thy sword,
> For all her cherubin look.
> [4.3.57–64]

Timon restates here the critical equation of war with lechery that Thersites makes in *Troilus and Cressida,* but does not do so in the idiom of the professional detractor whose satiric thrusts are indistinguishable from sarcasm. Rather, he speaks in the more authoritative vein of a self-exiled outsider who has become sufficiently estranged from the world he formerly inhabited to be able to anatomize its most common values and assumptions. Indeed, Timon "reads" the face of Alcibiades's "fell whore" with the same interpretive facility Macbeth brings to bear on the news of Lady Macbeth's death. And, though his insight into the cruelty of human institutions may be more sudden and unmediated than King Lear's, this is only the result of the dramatic shorthand Shakespeare employs throughout *Timon* to move his former concern with narrative development into the background, and to foreground what is most unaccommodating in his dramatic text.[21]

Surely, Timon *is* too wholesale in his condemnations, and Alcibiades does, conceivably, remain a more sympathetic character than Timon portrays. But this does not change the fact that most of what Timon asserts constitutes a faithful anatomy of the world the play presents and of the characters who inhabit it, as the following, consciously enigmatic exchange, seems meant to illustrate:

> *Alcib.* I have heard in some sort of thy miseries.
> *Tim.*   Thou saw'st them when I had prosperity.
> *Alcib.* I see them now; then was a blessed time.
> *Tim.*   As thine is now, held with a brace of harlots.
>
> [4.3.78–81]

Timon's attempt here to turn upside-down Alcibiades's notions about what constitutes misery and what constitutes prosperity meets with a complete lack of understanding on the part of a character presumably meant to embody our own normative notions about the same. This being the case, what, then, could Shakespeare have expected our own response to be? Clearly, Shakespeare would be asking as much of his audience as Timon is asking of Alcibiades were he to require it to reverse entirely its most ingrained notions about what *really* constitutes "a blessed time." The point is that Shakespeare *is* asking a lot of the audience, perhaps more than Timon (who knows very well that "then" had its share of blessings, as his later discourse on its "sweet degrees" makes plain) is asking of the irreversibly limited Alcibiades, who is more interested in Timon's gold than his "counsel" (4.3.131). Timon's baiting of Alcibiades seems intended to provoke the audience into making the kind of intellectual leap Alcibiades is plainly incapable of making; it seems meant to draw the audience out of its complacent identification with a set of values Timon is in the process of transvaluing. Shakespeare provides Timon with apt tools for his seemingly quixotic task by making the rest of Alcibiades's visit serve as the dramatic demonstration that his values are, indeed, "held with a brace of harlots." As the scene proceeds, and Phrynia and Timandra respond to Timon's injunction to "Be strong in whore" by saying, "Believe 't that we'll do anything for gold" (4.3.143, 152), our normative associations with Alcibiades are performatively broken down and displaced by the performatively more appealing spirit of indignation we identify with Timon, whose anatomy of the world now commands an enhanced admiration and respect.

This dramatic transaction (like others in the play, including

Timon's exchange with Apemantus) is, however, complicated
by the extreme form Timon's indignation takes and the unpre-
dictable effect of that form on an audience conceivably unac-
customed to identifying its interests with so harsh and unrelent-
ing a dramatic vehicle as invective:

> Consumptions sow
> In hollow bones of man; strike their sharp shins,
> And mar men's spurring. Crack the lawyer's voice,
> That he may never more false title plead,
> Nor sound his quillets shrilly. Hoar the flamen,
> That scolds against the quality of flesh,
> And not believes himself. Down with the nose,
> Down with it flat, take the bridge away
> Of him that, his particular to foresee,
> Smells from the general weal.
>
> [4.3.153–62]

Probably the most common strategy employed by playwrights
who wish to have their audience identify itself with a character
onstage is to make that character the walking embodiment of a
fantasy it too desires to see fulfilled. Such a character must be
able to awaken and bring to the surface impulses or aspirations
that an audience generally represses in its life outside the theater, and he must give these feelings at least the illusion of free
and unbridled play before it is time to tame or restrain them at
play's end. In this way the playwright provides his audience
with an area of licensed relief from the pressures of the quotidian, with a temporary escape from the limitations of its daily
round, and gives it an ephemeral, though sustaining, taste of
freedom and, even at times, omnipotence. In the end, to be
sure, plays that traffic in such effects—*Richard III* is an obvious
example—tend to insist on the illusoriness and illegitimacy of
such departures from the norm, and sometimes do so with a
fervor equal to the freedom their protagonists enjoy (e.g., Marlowe's *Doctor Faustus*). Usually, however, even such insistence is
less memorable than the fantasies that have been shared.[22]

In *Timon of Athens* Shakespeare seems to have set himself the
task of experimenting with and, in the process, complicating his
usual procedures. From the very start of the play, Timon's position in relation to the audience is made ambiguous. On the one
hand, he regales both on- and off-stage audiences with visions
of apparently unlimited abundance, and should, on that count
alone, provide for most of us the walking embodiment of our

dreams of wealth-in-idleness and for some a composite projection of an all-caring, all-providing, rather maternally inclined
father. On the other hand, Shakespeare makes a discernible
effort throughout the first act of the play to inhibit our impulse
to identify with Timon by warning us that "admiring Timon
the progidal is precisely what we are *not* intended to do."[23] This
warning is, moreover, conveyed as clearly by Timon himself as
it is by the sarcastic Apemantus, the concerned steward,
Flavius, and the flagrant insincerity of Timon's suitors. What
Terence Eagleton terms Timon's "projected egoism" generates
in performance the feeling that Timon's generosity is as remarkably self-satisfied and self-satisfying as it is ingratiating
and that it constitutes a characteristic gesture of self-
aggrandizement and exclusivity that seeks to invalidate the possibility of magnanimity in others.[24] As Timon says to Ventidius
as the latter attempts to repay a loan, "there's none / Can truly
say he gives, if he receives" (1.2.10–11), a remark Ventidius
seems to have expected, indeed, to have banked on, much as
Timon seems to expect from it a round of applause (which a
performance-minded reading of the ensuing nine lines suggests he gets, a standing ovation in fact). The pomposity of
Timon's liberality thus serves the purpose of undermining the
very fantasy he is originally meant to embody and of making it
an object of the audience's critical scrutiny. When Timon later
effects his dramatic transformation into a misanthropist, the
audience is consequently prepared to accept this reversal as the
logical realization of its own suspicions, as a turn in the performance the audience has anticipated and, perhaps, even desired. Compelled by the failure of the original fantasy to do
more than provoke its ambivalence, the audience plays a
cooperative role in the reformulation of that fantasy into more
immediately identifiable terms. This reformulated counterfantasy of misanthropy exploits the audience's cultivated distrust
in the duplicitous arrangements of society as the first three acts
of the play presents them, as well as its equally cultivated desire
to maintain its imaginative ties with a character who has at least
stimulated its capacity for identification and who now defines
himself in direct opposition to duplicity itself. The appeal of
this counterfantasy is communicated to the audience in the
most performatively immediate and unambivalent manner as
possible through the medium of invective, which supplies the
audience itself with the vicarious means to express its own

understandable resentment at the dissolution of its original terms of involvement with the play.

If we return now to the problem raised by Timon's insistent reversion to invective in the second half of the play, we may be better able to appreciate how a mode of speech that appears in the abstract to constitute a rather alienating approach to dramatic experience may, in performative terms, actually serve as the expressive vehicle of the audience's own interests. Clearly, a device such as hyperbole would seem to have more to recommend it than does invective in the context of a theater uniquely geared to raise an audience's sights above and beyond the struggles and pressures of the quotidian. But, as Burke contends, in a remarkably probing essay on *Timon*, invective may claim an appeal of its own that has not been as generally acknowledged as the appeal of hyperbole:

> *Invective*, I submit, is a primary "freedom of speech," rooted extralinguistically in the helpless rage of an infant that states its attitudes by utterances wholly unbridled. In this sense, no mode of expression could be more "radical," unless it be the closely allied motive of sheer *lamentation*, undirected wailing. . . .
> Obviously, the Shakespearean theater lends itself perfectly to the effects of invective. Coriolanus is an excellent case in point. Even a reader who might loathe his politics cannot but be engrossed by this man's mouthings. Lear also has a strong measure of such appeal, with his impotent senile maledictions that come quite close to the state of man's equally powerless infantile beginnings.[25]

Burke concludes his survey of Shakespeare's use of invective by stating that "with *Timon* the function [of invective] becomes almost total," and goes on to claim for Timon himself "a certain categorical or universal appeal," based mainly on his ability to give "full expression" to the impulse described.[26] Although I am unwilling to accept all of Burke's confident pronouncements at face value, I believe they strike at the heart of the prevailing critical difficulty with *Timon*, and are particularly useful in regard to the specific problem before us. For if, as Burke contends, invective has its source "in the helpless rage of an infant that states its attitudes by utterances wholly unbridled," in an emotion that refuses to accommodate itself to reason or restraint, how can we possibly expect to position ourselves in sympathetic relation to it? Clearly, we *cannot* sympathize in the theater with an emotion whose surface manifestations we would ordinarily find irritating outside the theater if the source

of that irritation is someone or something that we are indifferent to or alienated from. But we *can* sympathize with someone
or something that elicits or provokes—even against our will—
our capacity for identification, especially when the theatrical
apparatus itself has prepared us to make this apparent breach
in dramatic decorum the occasion for our own vicarious participation in the freedom from restraint it celebrates. As Burke
notes, Timon appeals to us, as Coriolanus and Lear appeal to us
despite the "practical discomfitures" engendered by their respective complaints, in large part because he indulges a freedom most of us have long ago suppressed in the face of "the
fears and proprieties that make up our 'second nature,'" a
nature dominated by an ethic of restraint.[27]

Viewed in the abstract, Timon's indulgence in this freedom
should be expected to garner little conscious support from an
audience conditioned by its "second nature" to relegate such
childish displays to the province of childish behavior. John Bayley speaks on behalf of such an audience when he states: "What
survives . . . in *Timon* is something *hurt,* and that is touching.
But how to relate it to the human scene?"[28] Shakespeare relates
it to the human scene by making the expression of the something that is "hurt" in *Timon* strike a responsive chord in the
something that is hurt, angry, or simply disappointed in all of
us, and by making that chord resonate with the play's concomitant attack on the very same "proprieties" that seek to hold our
responsiveness in conscious check. As the most extreme form
of unvarnished expression in which the play engages, invective
is geared to awaken in the audience that dormant "first nature"
which gives us access to feelings as unaccommodating as Timon's own, and thus to extend the range of our own emotional
involvement in Timon's expression of rage and resentment
against "the mendacious finery" of the world. Although, like
the drama within which it plays so crucial a role, invective may
not help either Timon or the audience "to accept loss," it may
well provide both with an expressive medium for the cathartic
release of feelings that do not necessarily require the "rituals of
atonement" theoretically considered mandatory for the
achievement of dramatic satisfaction.[29] As Burke suggests in a
related essay on *Coriolanus,* invective may actually serve a "curative function," consistent with its status as an idiom of denial
and refusal, when it is "released under controlled conditions

that transform the repressed into the expressed, yet do us no damage."[30]

In *Timon* invective operates within the "controlled conditions" of a dramatic experiment radical enough to encourage its audience to participate vicariously in the rejection of the audience's own "fears and proprieties," but sufficiently conventional to allow the audience to survive its own act of rejection after the object of its capacity for identification chooses to repress, once and for all, his capacity for self-expression: "Lips, let sour words go by and language end" (5.1.219).[31] Since Timon's renunciation of language occurs only after he has seemingly exhausted the resources of the medium through which his bond with the audience has been established, the audience should, conceivably, be purged of the impulses that made Timon its spokesman in the first place, and thus should be free to negotiate its way through the closing scenes of the play in a manner that is more consistent with its previously displaced normative persuasion. In the very scene in which Timon enacts his renunciation, Shakespeare has, however, taken pains to condition the audience to resist the movement toward accommodation that begins with the mercenary visit of the senators to Timon's cave and that culminates with Alcibiades's attempt to annex Timon's alienation to his questionable cause: "Those enemies of Timon's and mine own / Whom you yourselves shall set out for reproof / Fall, and no more" (5.4.56–58). We are treated in 5.1 to a striking extension of Timon's misanthropic idiom, to a flexibility of manner not generally associated with it, as he parodically plays upon the senators' accommodating rhetoric in his sarcastic response to the same blandishments that will soon win over the "wild" but more politic Alcibiades:

> You witch me in it;
> Surprise me to the brink of tears.
> Lend me a fool's heart and a woman's eyes,
> And I'll beweep these comforts, worthy senators.
>   [5.1.154–57]

And we are conspicuously reminded by Timon himself that he is as alienated from Alcibiades and his cause as he is from Athens and the senators who represent it: "Go, live still; / Be Alcibiades your plague, you his, / And last so long enough" (5.1.187–89).

Timon's refusal to enact the same compromise Alcibiades enacts in the play's closing scene may, of course, be construed in both psychological and ethical terms as a variety of regressive selfishness, of the kind we are meant to outgrow in the name of maturity. But in performative terms it operates as an influential determinant in shaping the way an audience will respond to Alcibiades's closing appeal to its second nature. Although humanity in the aggregate will do whatever it needs to do to protect itself from incursions against its safety and security, audiences at plays have little really to fear from theatrical assaults against their characteristic values and assumptions, and this is especially the case when the audience is actually encouraged to participate vicariously in a licensed release from normative constraints. In short, an audience may, in the closing moments of this play, experience more satisfaction in rejecting Alcibiades's attempt to dissolve the disruptive tensions provoked by Timon than it might experience were it to accept his formula for accommodation at face value. Alcibiades's alternative clearly promises the audience a smoother return to reality than does a continuing imaginative alliance with Timon's misanthropy. But it fails to offer the audience the final (though fleeting) luxury of feeling superior to a gesture the audience must soon perform in an analogous way of its own, as it reaccommodates itself to the values and standards of behavior that obtain outside the theater. Once it has sufficiently distanced itself from the affective range of theatrical experience, the audience will, presumably, come to acknowledge its essential resemblance to the normative likes of Alcibiades, and recognize the inescapable otherness of the abnormative Timon. But until the play ends, Alcibiades and the senators who attempt to appease him seem intended to serve as embodiments of what the audience imagines itself to be cured of, not as the welcome agents of a mutually desired reconciliation.

III

Having now claimed far more on behalf of *Timon* than it would seem reasonable to claim on behalf of a play that has elicited so many negative responses in the course of its critical history, it seems time to subject my own interpretive strategies to critical scrutiny. I have, in the preceding, developed a reading of a dramatic text based, for the most part, on what I have termed performative considerations. My reading has focused less on what the text means that on what it does or, more correctly, seems intended to do when it is performatively realized in immediate relation to an attentive and, perhaps, unusually responsive audience. I have, however, proceeded without reference either to a specific performance of *Timon,* or to an actual audience whose consensual responses to the sequences under examination could be accurately determined. My mode of approach has, instead, compelled me to construct a hypothetical version of *Timon* in performance that is consistent with the dramatic directives embedded in the playtext itself, and to reconstruct in both critical and descriptive terms the kinds of audience response such a version of the play would conceivably elicit. Both of these strategies are, of course, highly problematic. The version of *Timon* in performance I have constructed may represent as much of a distortion of the playtext's directives as anyone else's attempt to develop a performative model of the play, and may, moreover, be incapable of practical realization on the stage. And my critical reconstruction of audience response to a play I have myself set into motion may be too subjectively charged to lay any claim to consensual validity. The problem of consensual validity is, I believe, a central one, and has, in fact, provided the focus for many of the recent debates about the various forms of reader-response criticism, an enterprise that has much in common with the project I have undertaken here. Unfortunately, most proponents of reader-response criticism have confined themselves, both in theory and practice, to the consideration of texts whose performative function is completely "transacted" by the reader himself, in isolation from the powerful stimulus provided by actors on a stage and from the more subtle influence exerted by his membership in a company of consenting others.[32] In attempting to adapt the readerly persuasions of the likes of Norman Holland, Stanley Fish, and Wolfgang Iser to the specific demands of a dramatic text, it thus becomes necessary to begin by acknowledging the peculiar position that text holds in relation to the interpretive process.

Strictly speaking, the dramatic text operates as a supplement to the performance it plans or "maps," as a secondary source to a primary experience it closely resembles but with which it can never become synonymous. Transacting a reading with this text alone is, of course, a perfectly legitimate exercise insofar as the

performance to which the text refers can never be recon-
structed in a manner that will satisfy everyone in regard to its
validity or authority. However, no response to a dramatic text
that proceeds in the absence of performative considerations
can lay claim to being also a response to the *play* that is the
elusive signified of the textual signifier. This is the case because
a play performed in a uniquely public space, constructed with a
conscious regard for bringing audiences into close proximity to
speaking pictures and animated emotions, necessarily claims a
more active role in shaping and manipulating audience response than has recently been claimed for nondramatic texts,
which are considered to be mere passive accomplices to the
interpretive act itself.[33] This priority of performance dynamics
in a play's shaping of audience response requires the reader- or
audience-oriented critic of dramatic texts to construct a provisional mean between the two extremes embodied by the static
text which we alone can animate and the kinetic play which
alone can animate us. Lacking a representative performance
version of a play like *Timon* to which we can refer with the same
graphic consistency as we refer to its text, we are compelled to
operate in a middle ground that is, admittedly, of our own
making, but that is also shaped by a sustained regard for the
conventions of theatrical performance and for the peculiar psychology of theatrical experience. Obviously, the validity of this
operation finally depends on whether or not the audience-
oriented critic and *his* audience are in agreement in regard to
what these conventions are and what this peculiar psychology
actually entails; it depends, that is, on whether or not they
are—to borrow Fish's phrase—"member[s] of the same interpretive community."[34]

Although I am tempted to conclude, with Fish, that *my* audience "will agree with me . . . only if [it] already agree[s] with
me," I am equally tempted to believe that an exercise like the
one I have conducted in relation to *Timon of Athens* may be able
to provoke even the most wary of my readers to conduct similar
exercises of their own. I base my optimism on the fact that the
present generation of Shakespearean scholars and critics has
been for some time actively preoccupied with approaching the
plays of Shakespeare and his contemporaries as performance
texts, instead of as purely literary artifacts.[35] This emphasis on
performance values and dramatic conventions has, admittedly,
been generally restricted to the province of the stage itself;

scholars have wandered into the province of the audience only with the greatest reluctance and usually when they are well equipped with a stock of documentary sources.[36] Psychoanalytically inclined Shakespeareans have, of course, been more eager to project their own "identity themes" into the affective range of the audience, and it is with their critical procedures that my own approach to audience response is closely allied.[37] But in the end I am most interested in seeing whether a comparatively objective concern with Shakespeare in performance can be combined with a comparatively subjective concern for how performances are transacted by audiences in order to render a more complete model of theatrical experience than criticism has yet provided. Since my own model in this essay has been Burke's rather eclectic approach to *Timon*, I would like to conclude by summarizing his argument in the context of the issues I have raised above.

In claiming so privileged a position for Timon's commitment to invective in the dramatic economy of the play, and in suggesting that invective may serve a curative function for the audience that is usually associated with more decorous pronouncements on the part of Shakespeare's protagonists, Burke is both calling attention to the need to give priority to performance dynamics in the criticism of dramatic texts and confirming the priority of psychological effect, as opposed to "theme" or "meaning," in our experience of plays. Instead of standing back from the insistent presence of Timon himself in order to legislate a meaning consistent with Shakespeare's status as a humanistic institution—one that would presumably focus on Timon's prodigality, misplaced idealism, or downright immaturity—Burke grants Timon the dramatic status with which the play itself endows him, casting him as the prevailing focus of the play's theatrical gravity, as the sustained object of the play's operation on its audience's capacity for identification.[38] In so doing, he relieves us of our groundedness in a corrupt text that we attempt to piece together with the help of strategies borrowed from our experience of other, more obviously accommodating, plays, as well as from the stockpile of traditional literary criticism and received ideas. My own effort to give priority to the interplay between performance and response is meant to serve a similar function in regard to our general approach to other dramatic texts that are corrupt only insofar as they remain unanimated by performative considerations. At the very least, it is meant to encourage others to "Piece out [its] imperfections with [their] thoughts."

Notes

1. The quoted phrase is taken from Kenneth Burke, "*Timon of Athens* and Misanthropic Gold," in *Language as Symbolic Action* (Berkeley, Calif.: University of California Press, 1966), p. 115.

2. See, for example, G. Wilson Knight, "The Pilgrimage of Hate: An Essay on *Timon of Athens*," in *The Wheel of Fire*, 5th ed. (New York: Meridian Books, 1957), pp. 207–39. Knight actually takes his reading of the play beyond the bounds of my formulation by claiming that *Timon* constitutes "the archetype and norm of all tragedy" (p. 220).

3. See Susan Handelman, "*Timon of Athens:* The Rage of Disillusion," *American Imago* 36 (1979): 45–68, and Richard Fly, "Confounding Contraries: The Unmediated World of *Timon of Athens*," in *Shakespeare's Mediated World* (Amherst, Mass.: University of Massachusetts Press, 1976), pp. 117–42.

4. Norman Rabkin, *Shakespeare and the Common Understanding* (New York: The Free Press, 1967), p. 193.

5. Rabkin's manner of dismissing *Timon* may serve as a good example of Frederic Jameson's recent assertion that "the working theoretical framework or presuppositions of a given method are in general the ideology which that method seeks to perpetuate." The ideology within which Rabkin is working in *Common Understanding* would probably fall under the rubric of what Jameson terms "*ethical* criticism" or, more precisely, "metaphysical thought, which presupposes the possibility of questions about the 'meaning' of life"; see Jameson, *The Political Unconscious: Narrative as a Socially Symbolic Act* (Ithaca, N.Y.: Cornell University Press, 1981), pp. 58–60. For his part, Rabkin has recently revised his critical attitude toward "meaning"; he has, however, done so without sacrificing his commitment to humanistic ends which Jameson would consider ideologically exclusive as the following passage from *Shakespeare and the Problem of Meaning* (Chicago: University of Chicago Press, 1981) makes clear: "The challenge to criticism . . . is to embark on a self-conscious reconsideration of the phenomena that our technology has enabled us to explore, to consider the play as a dynamic interaction between artist and audience, to learn to talk about the process of our involvement rather than our considered view after the aesthetic event. We need to find concepts other than meaning to account for the end of a play, the sense of unverbalizable coherence, lucidity, and unity that makes us know we have been through a single, significant, and shared experience" (p. 27). Given his present emphasis on the process of audience involvement, it would appear doubtful that Rabkin would now endorse his earlier critical estimate of *Timon*.

6. *Timon*'s status as an experimental drama has already been noted by Una Ellis-Fermor, "*Timon of Athens:* An Unfinished Play," *Review of English Studies* 18 (1942): 270–83, and by Derek A. Traversi, *An Approach to Shakespeare*, vol. 2, 3d ed. (Garden City, N.Y.: Doubleday, 1969), p. 170. According to Ellis-Fermor, Shakespeare was, in *Timon*, "experimenting with structure; again, as in *Troilus and Cressida*, attempting a theme so original that the form it dictated must inevitably be revolutionary" (p. 275).

7. Handelman, "Rage of Disillusion," pp. 47–48.

8. See Jameson's discussion of the similarly accommodating impulses of "ethical" and psychological criticism in *Political Unconscious*, pp. 59–60.

CARTELLI: *TIMON OF ATHENS* 103

9. Handelman, "Rage of Disillusion," p. 48.

10. Cf. Jameson, *Political Unconscious:* "Here notions of personal identity, myths of the reunification of the psyche, and the mirage of some Jungian 'self' or 'ego' stand in for the older themes of moral sensibility and ethical awareness" (p. 60).

11. Although I accept here, for the sake of contrast, the conventional critical belief in the efficacy of the great tragedies in transforming the experience of loss into what Handelman terms "life-affirming energies," I believe it is in need of radical revision. The intensification of suffering that attends the closure of *King Lear*, for instance, probably does produce in some readers and most audiences an experience akin to Aristotelian catharsis. But do the closing colloquies of Kent, Albany, and Edgar really accommodate us to an acceptance of loss? Early redactors of Shakespeare did not appear to think so, and their sense of the original play as unrelievedly painful has been repeatedly echoed in our own time by scholars, directors, and filmmakers interested mainly in the play's seemingly unyielding pessimism.

12. Fly, "Confounding Contraries," p. 139.

13. Ibid., p. 125.

14. Ibid., p. 140.

15. Burke, "Misanthropic Gold," p. 119; Handelman, "Rage of Disillusion," p. 67.

16. Friedrich Nietzsche, *The Birth of Tragedy*, in *Basic Writings of Nietzsche*, ed. & trans. Walter Kaufmann (New York: Modern Library, 1968), p. 61.

17. All quotations from *Timon* are drawn from the Arden edition, ed. H. J. Oliver (London: Methuen, 1959).

18. Although I agree with Traversi in *An Approach to Shakespeare* that we should resist the temptation "to think of *Timon of Athens* as a kind of appendix to *King Lear*" and see it, instead, as an attempt on Shakespeare's part at "contriving a new kind of dramatic action" (p. 170), I believe that the aggressive, comparatively stripped-down dramatic orientation of the later play is a direct consequence of Shakespeare's continuing preoccupation with developing an appropriate language for tragic experience.

19. Traversi begins his own analysis of this scene (ibid., pp. 181–84) by stating that "the truth is evenly divided" between Timon and Apemantus, but concludes that "Timon remains distinguished from Apemantus by the ability to turn his life-weariness into distinctive poetry."

20. I have borrowed this terminology from Gabriele Bernhard Jackson's excellent article, "Structural Interplay in Ben Jonson's Drama," in *Two Renaissance Mythmakers*, ed. Alvin Kernan (Baltimore, Md.: Johns Hopkins University Press, 1977), pp. 113–45.

21. In purely narrative terms, it would make no sense to place Alcibiades in such company as he goes about the business of plotting his revenge against Athens. That Shakespeare has gone out of his way to make so explicit a connection between Alcibiades's martial pursuits and the whores' mercenary and "infectious" profession plainly suggests his endorsement of Timon's indictment.

22. I make this last point in relation to the closing movement of *Macbeth* in an article entitled "Banquo's Ghost: The Shared Vision," *Theatre Journal* 35, no. 3 (1983).

23. Anne Lancashire, "*Timon of Athens:* Shakespeare's *Doctor Faustus*," *Shakespeare Quarterly* 21 (1970): 42. Although I am in general agreement with what Lancashire has to say about Timon in regard to the first movement of the play (despite the fact that she seems blind to his obvious performance appeal), I disagree altogether with her overall reading of the drama, which derives from an oddly uncritical regard for its indebtedness to the morality tradition.

24. Terence Eagleton, "A Note on *Timon of Athens*," in *Shakespeare and Society* (New York: Schocken Books, 1967), pp. 172–76.

25. Burke, "Misanthropic Gold," p. 120.

26. Ibid., pp. 120–21.

27. Ibid., p. 121.

28. John Bayley, *Shakespeare and Tragedy* (London: Routledge & Kegan Paul, 1981), p. 87. I find Bayley's chapter on *Timon* (aptly entitled "The Big Idea") consistently illuminating and provocative and recommend it to anyone interested in a reading of the play opposed to the one provided here.

29. See Theodor Adorno's critique of what Wolfgang Iser terms the "quietistic aspect" of conventional psychological approaches to aesthetic experience: "The conformist acceptance by psychoanalysis of the popular view of art as beneficent to culture corresponds to aesthetic hedonism, which banishes all negativity from art, confining it to the conflicts that gave rise to the work and suppressing it from the end-product. If an acquired sublimation and integration are made into the be-all and end-all of the work of art, it loses that power through which it transcends the life which, by its very existence, it has renounced." Quoted in Iser, *The Act of Reading: A Theory of Aesthetic Response* (Baltimore, Md.: Johns Hopkins University Press, 1978), p. 47.

30. Kenneth Burke, "*Coriolanus*—and the Delights of Faction," *Language as Symbolic Action*, p. 94.

31. I have substituted the alternate reading "sour" in place of Oliver's choice of "four." Oliver defends his choice on the grounds that " 'sour' hardly makes sense, since Timon proceeds to further curses" (Arden edition, p. 132). I would suggest that it makes a great deal more sense than "four" since it announces the imminent, not simultaneous, termination of speech that, moreover, will be effected in *three lines*, instead of in the space of four words.

32. In employing the term "transacted," I am, of course, alluding to Norman Holland's psychoanalytically based models of reader response and, specifically, to a seminal work of his recent theoretical preoccupations, "Transactive Criticism: Re-Creation through Identity," *Criticism* 18 (1976): 334–52. In a more recent article, "How Can Dr. Johnson's Remarks on Cordelia's Death Add to My Own Response?", in *Psychoanalysis and the Question of the Text*, ed., Geoffrey H. Hartman (Baltimore, Md.: Johns Hopkins University Press, 1978), pp. 18–44, Holland directly addresses the problem of consensual validity in relation to what he terms the "outmoded and confusing" notion of "the 'power' of the text" (p. 40). Although they differ in several crucial ways in regard to the dynamics of reader response, Stanley Fish shares Holland's conception of the priority of the interpretive process. See, e.g., "Interpreting the *Variorum*," *Critical Inquiry* 2, no. 3 (1976): 465–85. Wolfgang Iser, on the other hand, claims a more significant role for the text itself in manipulating reader response and thus provides a supportive context for the argument I am attempting to make on behalf of dramatic texts. See *The Act of Reading*, pp. 152–53.

33. Cf. Fish, in "Interpreting the *Variorum*": "In my model . . . meanings are not extracted but made and made not by encoded forms but by interpretive strategies that call forms into being" (p. 485).

34. Ibid.

35. Examples range from Bernard Beckerman's seminal *Shakespeare at the Globe* (New York: Macmillan, 1962) and J. L. Styan's *Shakespeare's Stagecraft* (Cambridge: Cambridge University Press, 1967) to Michael Goldman's "applied" readings of Shakespeare's texts in *Shakespeare and the Energies of Drama* (Princeton, N.J.: Princeton University Press, 1972).

36. The latest and, to my mind, most illuminating study of Shakespeare's audience is Ann Jennalie Cook's *The Privileged Playgoers of Shakespeare's London* (Princeton, N.J.: Princeton University Press, 1981).

37. See Norman Holland, "Unity Identity Text Self," *PMLA* 90 (1975): 814. Also see Murray M. Schwartz and Coppelia Kahn, eds., *Representing Shakespeare: New Psychoanalytic Essays* (Baltimore, Md.: Johns Hopkins University Press, 1980).

38. For a British version of the present argument, see Derek Longhurst's examination of Shakespeare's treatment as "the National Poet," " 'Not for all time, but for an Age': An Approach to Shakespeare Studies," in *Re-Reading English,* ed. Peter Widdowson (London: Methuen, 1982), pp. 150–63.

Rousseau's Narrative Strategies for Readers of His Autobiographical Works

John C. O'Neal

Hamilton College

I N his autobiographical works, Rousseau attempts to render the truest possible image of himself. The image that he presented, however, was not always properly understood by his eighteenth-century public. Rousseau recognized the problems attendant to receiving either visual or verbal images and naturally attributed them to a certain blindness in himself as well as in those for whom he wrote. Since Enlightenment sensationalism gave primacy to visual perception as a major basis for epistemological certitude, Rousseau began writing about himself in a literary form by which he sought to elicit a desired intuitive mode of seeing. But his writings ultimately lead him to offer reading rather than any mode of seeing as the best guide to a clear understanding of his image. This analysis generally leaves aside the considerable relationship between Rousseau and a within (himself) and a without (others) in order to focus on the relationship between others and a within (themselves) and a without (Rousseau). In short, the point of view under scrutiny here is that of an eighteenth-century observer or reader, seen both as an individual and as a member of society. Rousseau's ultimate solution to the problems of self-representation can perhaps best be grasped by first elaborating the presuppositions he makes about his readers' frequent perceptual inadequacies.

According to Rousseau, other people manifest their own incapacity to see in two primary ways that he assumes of any observer or reader. Either they look through others' eyes, relying merely on public opinion, or they see only themselves in someone else, and in so doing confuse their projections of themselves for the other person. Acutely sensitive to sometimes real, sometimes self-delusive slander, Rousseau directs himself to what he considers its causes. If only others could see him as he truly is, they would understand him and cease perpetrating inaccurate remarks about him. Unfortunately, the public prefers increasingly to trust the observations of a small number of people who persist in holding grave misconceptions over his character. For the increasingly paranoid Rousseau, this small group of people, whose principal leaders he believes to find in Grimm and Diderot, constitutes a "league" that is plotting to disfigure his image through their influence on public opinion.[1] Since these people occupy influential positions in society, Rousseau decides that he must counteract their vilification of him. In *Les Confessions* and *Les Dialogues,* he assembles his defense, which rests largely upon the invalidation of their perceptual gauge.[2]

As the tension rises around him, Rousseau comes to feel that the group's efforts have proved successful. People forsake seeing through their own eyes and rely more and more on the league's, as the fictional "Rousseau"[3] relates to the "Frenchman" in *Les Dialogues:*

> This change of opinion appears very natural to me without furnishing the proof that you draw from it. They used to see him then through their own eyes, they have seen him since through those of others. You think that they were mistaken in the past; personally I believe that it is today that they are mistaken. I see no solid reason at all in your opinion, and I see one of great weight in my own; it is that then there was no league and that today there is one. [*Dial.*, p. 775]

Perhaps nothing irritates Rousseau more than the partisan spirit he sees around him. When directed at him, it becomes particularly distasteful, for in his case it is used to modify others' perception of him. The Frenchman gives a hypothetical example: "If d'Alembert or Diderot on a whim affirmed today that he has two heads, upon seeing him go by in the street tomorrow everyone would see him very distinctly with two heads" (*Dial.*, p. 961). In France, Rousseau distinguishes a court party and a philosophical one, both of which, he says, oppose him. He concludes:

> In general any party man, by that association alone an enemy of truth, will always hate J.J. . . . . Now there is never in these collective bodies any disinterested love for justice: nature has only engraved it in the hearts of individuals, where it is soon extinguished by the league's mentality. [*Dial.*, p. 965]

As long as people subscribe to someone else's preordained ideas, they will remain unaware of truth and justice. And hate, often and not surprisingly called blind, becomes the primary manifestation of a partisan spirit.

Society, in its tendency toward partisanship, brings about a reversal in the primitive individual. Hate substitutes itself for love, and the league for the individual, in much the same way that *amour-propre* (selfish love) does for *amour de soi* (love of self). In describing the degradation of man, Rousseau employs a rhetoric that abounds with terms evocative of a cataclysm. Medically speaking, it attains the proportions of an epidemic. "Rousseau" explains to the Frenchman:

> there are, so to speak, epidemics of the mind that overtake men step by step as would a kind of contagion; because the naturally lazy human mind likes to spare itself pain by following the thoughts of others especially in that which flatters its own tendencies. [*Dial.*, p. 880]

Man has a natural tendency toward indolence. The league exploits that tendency in order to have him see and read the way the group does.

"Jean-Jacques,"[4] the subject of a kind of Platonic elenchus in *Les Dialogues*, thus serves in real life as the object of others' gazes, motivated not out of love but out of a hate directed by the league. All that is selfish love gives over to unbridled abhorrence. It suffices to compare oneself to the supposedly vice-ridden Jean-Jacques in order to feel immaculate. A direct function exists between the perception of one's own well-being and that of Jean-Jacques's depravity. In *Les Dialogues*, the

Frenchman represents one of *autrui*, one of the "others," who has fallen prey to the dark practices of the league and who has become insidiously enmeshed in partisan spirit, selfish love, and comparison. "Rousseau," his interlocutor, berates him and, at the same time, all members of society who become at moments unmindful of the dangers they run in their world:

> You found a bad side to everything that came from that hapless man and a good side to everything that tended to slander him; the acts of perfidy, the betrayals, the lies lost all their darkness in your eyes when he was the object of them, and provided that you not become involved in them yourself you had grown accustomed to seeing them without horror in other people: but what was in you only a passing distraction has become for the public an habitual delirium, a constant principle of behavior, an universal jaundice, the fruit of a bitter and widespread bile, which alters not only the sense of sight but also corrupts all the humors and finally kills entirely the moral man who would have remained of sound constitution without it. [*Dial.*, p. 881]

Rousseau's appraisal of his predicament is clear. The public has contracted an epidemic jaundice that not only damages its physical apparatus but also its ability to feel with inner conviction. In effacing these two essential elements, this sickness altogether dismantles the public's capacity to "see." What perception is left consists merely in "observing," which will not yield a true picture of Jean-Jacques and which, furthermore, reinforces those very forces that foster insensitivity.

The eyes trained upon Rousseau and his texts belong, therefore, not to the individual, but to the group. A handful of people have tricked the public; "when they believe that they are seeing through their eyes, they are seeing, without suspecting it, through the eyes of other people" (*Dial.*, p. 896). Rousseau shudders at the prospect of this collective gaze. He always shuns the large assembly in favor of the tête-à-tête, where the individual across from him is more prone to use the wealth of his own resources to see and not rely on other people's perception.

Blindness also occurs, as noted above, on the level of the individual. When merely able to see oneself in someone else, one's own person obstructs an otherwise clear understanding of the other. In Rousseau's mind, others fail to recognize him for what he is because of his uniqueness. They insist unwittingly upon transposing to Rousseau their own undesirable qualities.

The sordid image of Jean-Jacques becomes, then, a reflection of themselves and of all the evil spawned in them. They presume to see and measure accurately the true Rousseau, but they only succeed in so doing for themselves, not him. Rousseau is "other." Quite simply, he is not they. But they refuse to believe this fundamental distinction and remain "obstinate in always judging [him] by themselves" (*Conf.*, p. 644). In the Neuchâtel manuscript of *Les Confessions*, Rousseau comments at length upon the phenomenon:

> I have often noticed that, even among those who pride themselves the most on knowing men, each one scarcely knows but himself, if it is true even that someone might know himself; because how does one really determine a being by the relationships that alone are in himself, and without comparing him with anything? This imperfect knowledge that one has of himself, however, is the only means that one uses to know other people. One makes of himself the rule for everything, and that is precisely where the double illusion of selfish love awaits us; either in attributing falsely to those whom we judge the motives that would have made us act as they did in their situation; either in this very supposition, by abusing ourselves about our own motives, through our incapacity to know how to put ourselves enough into another situation than the one in which we are.[5]

This passage underlines an inherent inability to see or to know anyone other than oneself. Man is cut off, alienated from others and must consequently grope about with his "antennae." He may be the measure of all things, but how well does he really know other things or other people? At best, he only knows himself and even that, imperfectly. It is in this sense of being almost prisoners of ourselves that we become numb to others. If Rousseau writes indefatigably about himself, it is precisely because in so doing he can justly claim to abide by the truth. Only he can fathom those nether regions of his self, *intùs, et in cute*, and present its depth.[6] Others' libels against him thus come to reinforce in his mind their benightedness. And even when they represent him in a kind way, they still remain unaware of their mistake: "Learned men in the art of feigning / Who attribute to me such soft features / You will want in vain to paint me, / You will never paint but yourselves" (*Dial.*, p. 778).

The mind attempts to compensate for man's shortcomings, for his failure to know adequately someone else. Its efforts, however, are aimed more at self-indulgence than true understanding. Rousseau tersely resumes: "one wants to guess, one wants to be penetrating; it is the natural game of selfish love: one sees what one believes and not what one sees" (*Dial.*, p. 742). If others used their reasoning faculty properly, they might more closely approximate the true image of Rousseau. But they fall prey to the negative trappings of observing in a rational way. When they do consult their "inner light" rather than all too easily accepting another's judgment, they do not perceive from a disinterested viewpoint, but from a selfish one. Others neglect to use suitably their intellectual powers. Nor do they take full advantage of the possibilities afforded by their conscience. Their reflection upon Rousseau as an object does not entail a happy introspection. Whereas Rousseau relates to others through the within,[7] they choose to view him in one of two ways. Either they look through others' eyes or they try to see through an *amour-propre* that restricts their field of vision by superimposing their qualities on someone else.

Mental operations as well as ones induced by feeling can transcend the distance between a subject and an object. But the soul must expand in order to promote intersubjective communication. As long as it stays preoccupied with selfish love, no illumination will ever come, according to Rousseau. But if this blight can be removed, clarity of vision will astonish everyone. And it is this enlightened age that Rousseau earnestly wants to usher in: "As soon as passion and prejudice will cease to be fostered, a thousand things that one does not notice today will strike all eyes" (*Dial.*, p. 970).

In the face of others' inability to see or observe him properly, Rousseau must devise another cognitive model.[8] Rousseau may attempt indirectly to bring about change on a larger scale, but his more immediate concern in his later years is with the public's image of him. *Les Confessions* and particularly *Les Dialogues* deal specifically with changing that image. As he approaches his last hour, Rousseau becomes anxious over the reputation he will leave for posterity. Unless he succeeds in changing the portrait that others have painted of him in his own generation, he will remain a "monster" for the ones to come. It is *Les Dialogues* that continue and largely conclude the elucidating task initiated in *Les Confessions*. In the conversations between "Rousseau" and the Frenchman, the maligned author seeks to bring about an approximate coincidence of what *is* and what is seen or read.

Aware of his project's immensity, Rousseau chooses the

fictional mode, and, like Plato, the dialogue. Through its dialec-
tical nature, the dialogue lends itself more readily to the representation of pure form. In *Les Dialogues* the two characters establish early on a fundamental distinction concerning "Jean-
Jacques." There are two Jean-Jacques, one a criminal, the other
a virtuous person. Whereas the Frenchman unites them in the
same person, "Rousseau," who has read his books, separates
them. He sees their author as a pious man and cannot reconcile
that person with the author of the alleged, heinous crimes.
Hence, "Rousseau," unlike the Frenchman, refuses to judge
entirely Jean-Jacques without having seen him first with his
own eyes. The one demands immediate evidence, the other
only hearsay proof. "Rousseau" elaborates:

> if I had not seen deception where you claim to see evidence, this
> evidence at least has disappeared so much from my eyes, that in
> everything that you have demonstrated to me I no longer see but an
> insolvable problem, a frightening and impenetrable mystery that
> the conviction of the guilty person alone can clarify in my eyes.
> [*Dial.*, p.730]

He must see Jean-Jacques in person and hear his testimony
before he can make a decision. The Frenchman, on the other
hand, contents himself with reading the author's books before
rendering an opinion.

"Rousseau"'s solution to visit Jean-Jacques in order to acquire enough information to judge him adequately circum-
vents the problem of seeing through others' eyes. But inherent
difficulties crop up in his plan when he proposes to see Jean-
Jacques as he actually is, not as he thinks or imagines him to be.
Acts of thought and imagination relate to the individual and
thereby constitute unacceptable evidence for "Rousseau," who
is seeking information outside of himself. He must confront the
problem of his own blindness. But what can he use, then, to
deliver the essence of Jean-Jacques's being? Who is Jean-
Jacques? "Rousseau" may look with his own eyes upon him, but
do the resulting images or sensations truly represent Jean-
Jacques? The greater question that examines the possibility of
any true perception is treated on the individual level of one
single person: how does one truly know Jean-Jacques? A response to this question brings us to the domain proper of autobiography.

Autobiography holds up a single object for observation. Here it is Jean-Jacques Rousseau. He will become an index for his own clarity of vision as well as theirs. The degree to which he and they can make true statements about him will determine their respective clear-sightedness. In looking upon him, others should be able easily to see the true Jean-Jacques. And yet the portrait they paint of him cannot but vary with his own. Whereas everything Rousseau says in analyzing himself theoretically yields the unity of the perceived object, others are always at odds over what they see. The notion to which Rousseau resorts in describing others' vision invariably centers around disparity. Their vision yields disparity; his, unity. As a group of onlookers, they can never obtain the overview necessary to produce a unified image. Their multiple gazes have no common denominator, no constitutive ego or soul.

Mon Portrait gives voice to this lack of a commonly held perceptual basis in others: "All the copies of a same original resemble one another, but have the same face drawn by various painters, hardly will all these portraits have the slightest relationship between them."[9] Furthermore, Rousseau himself avows his ever-changing nature that requires more than one simple glance and thereby compounds others' perception of him. But each individual can gather a clear picture of Rousseau by reading about his life in all its various facets. Paradoxically, the movement for others is from the Many to the One, and for Rousseau from the One to the Many. The obligation is thus two-fold: one, on the part of Rousseau to expose in his narration all sides of his self; the other, that of the reader to consider (that is, read) all the different parts of Rousseau to establish the whole. Nor is a perfect accomplishment of both tasks without its own obvious snares for those concerned.

The task that Rousseau imposes upon himself binds him to perhaps the truest form of autobiography. He is not going to narrate only those aspects of himself that he finds most flattering but all parts so that the reader can eventually construct his unity:

I would like to be able in some way to make my soul transparent to the eyes of the reader, and for that I seek to show it to him from *all points of view,* to throw light on it through every day, to proceed in such a way that there occurs not one movement that he does not notice, so that he can judge by himself the principle that produces them. [*Conf.,* p. 175]

Rousseau's unity comes to us through the multiplicity of his character. When directed upon himself, each one of his gazes attains a kind of basic truth. He presages by almost a century the celebrated dictum for Kierkegaard: "truth is subjectivity."[10] Yet when others look upon Rousseau, no one of their glances approximates the same truth. They must take recourse to an empirical method that will give them in the long run a truer image of Rousseau. All too often, however, they stop short of this image, which requires exceedingly close attention and much time. They then produce a "monster" whose "heterogeneous parts . . . by their number, their disproportion, their incompatibility, could not possibly form a whole" (*Dial.*, p. 746).

Rousseau loathes the disparity that results from others' partial observation of him. He never quite appreciates any portrait that others paint of him. Inevitably something is overlooked or something is added (as Saint-Preux discovers upon receiving Julie's portrait in *La Nouvelle Héloïse*). Others not only represent Rousseau partially, but also disfigure him. Ramsay's portrait, he thinks, turns him into a cyclops (*Dial.*, p. 780). The only authentic portrait must come from Rousseau himself, as he states in his *Lettres à Malesherbes:*

> I shall paint myself without make-up, and without modesty, I shall show myself to you as I see myself, and as I am, because spending my life with myself I must know myself and I see by the manner in which those who think that they know me, interpret my actions, and my behavior that they know nothing about them. No one in the world knows me but I alone.[11]

His written portrait will also be a copy of the original that defies absolute presentation, but it will at least resemble it.

When Rousseau narrates his early life, he takes pain to note on several occasions the recurrence of false judgments made about him. In Geneva, M. Masseron bemoans Rousseau's seemingly total ineptitude. At Annecy, M. d'Aubonne, upon Mme de Warens' beckoning, agrees to examine Rousseau only to conclude with an endorsement of M. Masseron's pronouncement. In his waning years, with increasing ambiguity surrounding his image, Rousseau turns more and more to the task of definitively rectifying the record. He needs others to see him as he really is. He alone must give his portrait, since others have all too often misunderstood him. The wealth of autobiographical works in his later years attests to the urgency Rousseau felt, despite his express desire to quit writing, to produce the truest image possible of himself. Rousseau must undergo his own examination.[12]

Rousseau's self-examination asserts itself as nothing less than a self-analysis, the process of which has rarely, if ever, been performed successfully even unto our own day. (It can be said, for instance, that even Freud never actually attempted or achieved an unequivocal analysis of himself.)[13] In autobiography when one deals strictly with oneself, the patient-analyst relationship is lacking: there can be no transference.[14] For his proposed task, Rousseau must assume the role of both patient and analyst or he must attempt total introspection. He must either entirely rationally observe or "lucidly" see himself. The one form of perception yields a pure object; the other, a pure subject. And yet man can neither be a complete object nor subject to himself. "Rousseau" does examine "Jean-Jacques," but only on a fictional basis. As Jean Starobinski notes: "The perfect doubling or the entire adhesion to one's self, are extreme states toward which the consciousness orients itself with obstination, but that it never attains."[15] Rousseau, or the true Jean-Jacques, the much sought-after referent of the dialogue, is not to be found among the pages of *Les Dialogues*. Nor does there ever occur an identification of narrator and author in any literature.[16] In attempting to analyze himself in his autobiographical writings, Rousseau, by an ironic turn, wants to underline not the authenticity of his own gaze and narrative, but their lies. If we are to understand Rousseau's self-portraits, we must consider them above all for their fictional value and not their real one. As narratives, they function well precisely because they do not represent and are not mimetic.[17]

One of the foremost objectives of his writing consists in giving his readers what he calls "a comparison piece" for their lives. The Neuchâtel manuscript of *Les Confessions* states this quite forcefully:

> Upon these remarks I have resolved to have my readers take one more step in the knowledge of men, by pulling them away if possible from that sole and faulty rule of judging always another's heart by one's own; whereas on the contrary it would often be necessary in order to know one's own, to begin by reading in another's. I want to proceed in my task in such a way that others might be able to have at least one comparison piece in order to learn to appreciate themselves; that each one be able to know himself and one other person, and I will be this other person.[18]

Doubtless, all Rousseau's autobiographical writings point out
to others events and situations that changed him, and thereby
indirectly invite others to reflect upon the events of their own
lives with the hopeful goal of bettering them.[19] In this sense,
Rousseau composes with his autobiographies a kind of *Morale
sensitive* without the title. But above all, these works are designed to encourage others to make another positive comparison. Rousseau wants to stress the lie involved in speaking about
oneself, and what is much more, speaking about someone else.
If his own works are fictitious, then their representations of
him are doubly so. Other men only begin to know themselves
when they realize how difficult a task self-knowledge is. Rousseau's writings become in this way a bible for self-analysis. If
others read Rousseau and understand his failure to achieve
what he is seeking, that is, a gaze turned upon himself, then
they will have made one step on the road to wisdom.

The point remains, however, that Rousseau emphasizes *reading* and not seeing. In *Les Dialogues* "Rousseau" goes off to see
Jean-Jacques at the conclusion of his first conversation with the
Frenchman, who promises to read Jean-Jacques's works. His
firsthand examination of "Jean-Jacques" supposedly will give
him solid evidence as to his true character. But knowing does
not necessarily equal seeing, as Jean-Jacques's answer to "Rousseau" indicates:

"You are the first person to arrive here guided by his own motives:
because of so many people who have the curiosity to *see* me, not one
has the curiosity to know me; everyone believes that he knows me
well enough. Come then, for the rarity of the occurrence. But what
do you want from me, and why speak to me of my books? If after
you have *read* them, they could leave you in doubt about the feelings of the Author, do not come: in that case I am not your man,
because you could not possibly be mine." [*Dial.*, pp. 776–77]

Rousseau, the author, gives one to believe that his truest portrait exists in his writings and not in the actual image of him
that comes from immediate observation. If "Rousseau" does
not recognize the truth of Jean-Jacques's fictional image, he will
glean little from scrutinizing him in person. We rejoin here
some ideas concerning love from *La Nouvelle Héloïse.* In the
same way that Saint-Preux's truest image of Julie resides in his
heart and imagination, the truest picture of Rousseau resides in
his autobiographical works as they take on the air of fiction and
the land of chimera.

An incredulous "Rousseau" notes the difficulty of seeing Jean-Jacques even once he is right upon him: "I had reached his person, but so many difficulties remained for me to overcome in the way in which I was proposing to examine him!" (*Dial.*, p. 782). The thorny points are raised once again: seeing through others' eyes, and not being able to see outside of oneself. Perception tends to give ambiguous sensations that do not reveal the true Jean-Jacques. "Rousseau" expresses the desire "to observe him less by equivocal and rapid signs than by his constant manner of being; the sole, infallible rule for properly judging a man's true character and the passions he might hide in the bottom of his heart" (*Dial.*, pp. 783–84). The final difficulty, however, becomes one not so much of seeing per se, but of reading. It is reading that yields finally that "constant manner of being," the constant image, one that comes to us, however, not synchronically or at a glance as in sensory perception but diachronically or across time.

When properly undertaken with the heart as a guide, reading endows us with perhaps optimal vision in that it delivers the truest image of Jean-Jacques. "Rousseau" remarks about men in general: "Paying too much attention to their speeches and not enough to their works, I would listen to them speak rather than watch them act" (*Dial.*, p. 783). His statement seems, of course, to establish the primacy of gestures over spoken languages, and of acts over speech. Actually, the statement by "Rousseau" paradoxically reinstates the validity of written language and aesthetic representation. As Jacques Derrida has pointed out, an absence (language in its supplementary relationship to referents) can serve to restore a presence (here, the self.)[20] I dwell over the word *oeuvres* in that it evokes not only the acts of Rousseau's life but also the actual literary works that represent them. As acts, these latter, and not the true-life events, give the final word.

When "Rousseau" becomes pressed to give an *idée sommaire* or comprehensive idea (*Dial.*, p. 797) of Jean-Jacques, his very own remarks have their place in a fictional text. Neither "Rousseau" nor anyone else can totalize all the images of Jean-Jacques in reality. During his lifetime, Rousseau can actually *show* himself to others for them to see. But it is really only when he *tells* of his life in a narrative so that others may read him that he truly allows himself to be seen.[21] In Rousseau's later years, his presence as a writer becomes more important than his visible presence. By choosing autobiography earlier, Rousseau

hoped that this literary form would most closely approximate
actual perception through the projection of an image that
would put the reader in touch with an aspect of what was being
represented—the thing in itself—and, by extension, its true
nature. Yet the transition from *Les Confessions* to *Les Dialogues*
follows Rousseau's increasing predilection for a more fictional
mode of writing about the self and a less perceptually based
mode of reading that might attempt to circumscribe synchronically the author in a single image.

By virtue of aesthetic and temporal factors, truth resides
more in the narration of a life than in a perception of it. Rousseau's narrative about himself reveals his temporal and spatial
limitations, that is, to what extent he, like any narrator in
fiction, "does not 'know' simultaneously but consecutively."[22] It
is precisely the consecutive images he presents of himself and
his awareness of the differences between them that allow Rousseau to recognize the fiction of any image frozen in time. The
reader, however, can seize the truth, which indeed is in the tale.
The basis of truth shifts in Rousseau's time from the *évidence*
(that is, the certitude that comes from perception) hallowed by
the eighteenth century to the evidence of fiction. As Michel
Foucault notes about a similar change in medicine at the end of
the century: "A way of teaching and *saying* became a way of
learning and *seeing*."[23] Although "Rousseau," who has seen
Jean-Jacques, gives the last few words of the text, it is the
Frenchman, he who has just read Jean-Jacques's works recently
and on two separate occasions (the second of which being a very
detailed and careful reading), who dominates the third and last
of *Les Dialogues*. He does not need to see Jean-Jacques. His
decision to content himself only with what he has read should
not be taken too lightly.

Notes

1. In its attempts to explain behavioral disorders, psychoanalysis has found highly
significant the initial moment an infant sees himself in a mirror as a *Gestalt*. Subsequent
modifications of such a specular image through socialization produce varying degrees
of paranoid alienation. See Jacques Lacan, "Le stade du miroir comme formateur de la
fonction du je, telle qu'elle nous est révélée dans l'expérience psychanalytique," *Revue
Française de Psychanalyse* 13, no. 4 (1949): 449–55. One is reminded of the mirror
imagery in Rousseau's play *Narcisse*.
2. Jean-Jacques Rousseau, *Les Confessions* and *Rousseau juge de Jean-Jacques* or *Les*

Dialogues in *Oeuvres complètes*, vol. 1 (Paris: Gallimard, 1959). Hereafter, I refer to these editions as *Conf.* and *Dial.* Page references are included in the text. All italics in the Rousseau quotations as well as all translations of them and unattributed French texts are mine. I have abbreviated Rousseau's *Oeuvres complètes* in the Pléiade edition as *OC*. Most of Rousseau's major autobiographical works, with the notable exception of his *Rêveries du promeneur solitaire*, are dealt with here. This latter work, it was felt, presented too unique a problem in its author's avowed lack of concern about the reader to be grouped with the other autobiographical writings being analyzed.

3. Remarks made about "Rousseau" refer specifically to the fictional character of *Les Dialogues*.

4. Subsequent references herein to Jean-Jacques or "Jean-Jacques" are specifically to the much slandered, problematic, fictional character of *Les Dialogues*, not to Rousseau himself.

5. *OC*, 1, "Ébauches des Confessions," p. 1148.

6. Rousseau's use of the written word to display the depth of his soul echoes the argument advanced by the Abbé du Bos in the early eighteenth century that the painter's area of expertise is *di fuori* while the poet's is *di dentro*. See Rensselaer W. Lee, *Ut Pictura Poesis: The Humanistic Theory of Painting* (New York: Norton, 1967), p. 61.

7. The process will reverse itself somewhat in *Les Rêveries* as Rousseau moves more freely from without to within.

8. This is, of course, the model of reading, which has been explored somewhat by Christie V. McDonald. See "The Model of Reading in Rousseau's *Dialogues*," *Modern Language Notes* 93 (1978): 723–32. My essay attempts to illuminate how this new model comes to have, as a last resort, epistemological superiority over any mode of perception. I hasten to emphasize, however, as does McDonald, that reading is not without its distortions either. Another useful work on the act of reading in Rousseau is Robert J. Ellrich's *Rousseau and His Reader: The Rhetorical Situation of the Major Works* (Chapel Hill, N.C.: University of North Carolina Press, 1969).

9. *OC*, 1, pp. 1121–22.

10. Søren Kierkegaard, "Concluding Unscientific Postscript to the 'Philosophical Fragments,'" trans. David F. Swenson, Lillian Marvin Swenson and Walter Lowrie, in *A Kierkegaard Anthology*, ed. Robert Bretall (New York: Modern Library, 1946), pp. 190–258.

11. *OC*, 1, p. 1133.

12. For a treatment of self-portraits in seventeenth- and eighteenth-century French literature, see Jean Rousset, *Narcisse romancier. Essai sur la première personne dans le roman* (Paris: Corti, 1973), esp. pp. 37–47, 103–13.

13. Jean Laplanche and J.-B. Pontalis, *Vocabulaire de la psychanalyse* in *L'Autobiographie en France*, ed. Philippe Lejeune (Paris: Colin, 1971), pp. 251–53.

14. Ibid., pp. 92–93.

15. Jean Starobinski, *L'Oeil vivant* (Paris: Gallimard, 1961), p. 168.

16. Michel Butor, *Essais sur le roman* (1964; reprint ed., Paris: Gallimard, 1975), p. 76. Structural analysis reaffirms the imperative that author and narrator not be confused. See Roland Barthes, "Introduction to the Structural Analysis of Narratives," in *Image-Music-Text*, trans. Stephen Heath (New York: Hill and Wang, 1977), pp. 111–14.

17. Barthes, *op. cit.*, pp. 123–24.

18. *OC*, 1, p. 1149.

19. If the reader is not merciful or does not become so in reading Rousseau's autobiographies, he has overlooked one of their more profound didactic elements. These works provide moving lessons in man's blindness. For an analysis of the ways in which

an author may evoke virtuous behavior from the reader, see *Reader-Response Criticism: From Formalism to Post-Structuralism,* ed. Jane P. Tompkins (Baltimore, Md.: Johns Hopkins University Press, 1980). In summarizing some of the articles by contributors to the collection of essays she has edited (pp. xv–xvi), Tompkins notes that "to adopt a particular conception of the reader is to engage in a particular kind of virtuous action—the refining of one's moral sensors (Gibson), adding to the sum of human knowledge (Prince), coming ever closer to the truth through attention to linguistic detail (Riffaterre), achieving self-transcendence through self-effacement (Poulet), or building a better self through interpretive enterprise (Iser)."

20. See Jacques Derrida, *De la grammatologie* (Paris: Éditions de Minuit, 1967), esp. chap. 2, "Ce Dangereux Supplément," pp. 203–34. For another deconstructionist reading of Rousseau, see also Paul de Man, *Allegories of Reading: Figural Language in Rousseau, Nietzsche, Rilke, and Proust* (New Haven, Conn.: Yale University Press, 1979), esp. pp. 278–301.

21. For a somewhat different use of the terms *showing* and *telling* in narrative technique, cf. Wayne C. Booth, *The Rhetoric of Fiction* (Chicago: University of Chicago Press, 1961), chap. 1, "Telling and Showing," pp. 3–20 and chap. 8, "Telling and Showing: Dramatized Narrators, Reliable and Unreliable," pp. 211–40.

22. Robert Scholes and Robert Kellogg, *The Nature of Narrative* (New York: Oxford University Press, 1966), p. 272.

23. Michel Foucault, *The Birth of the Clinic: An Archaeology of Medical Perception,* trans. A. M. Sheridan Smith (New York: Vintage Books, 1975), p. 64; Foucault's emphasis. See also pp. 114 and 195.

Thoreau's Composition of the Narrator: From Sexuality to Language

Ross J. Pudaloff

Wayne State University

In a transcendental philosophy, where everything depends on freeing form from content and keeping what is necessary clear from everything fortuitous, we too easily become accustomed to think of the material simply as a hindrance, and to represent the sense faculty as necessarily opposed to reason because in this particular matter it stands in our way.

Schiller, On The Aesthetic Education of Man, In a Series of Letters

In short, the subject (and its substitutes) must be stripped of its creative role and analysed as a complex and variable function of discourse.

Michel Foucault, "What Is An Author?"

I

THOREAU lived and participated in the age and literary movement that originated the term *psychological* precisely when and because the concept of the self had become both problematical and important. But he shared with Coleridge, who coined the word in *Aids to Reflection*, the conviction that it was an *insolens verbum*, the problem of the times rather than the glory of the literature. To read his work, then, even and especially the *Journals*, as the expression of unmediated fears, fantasies, dreams, and desires, is a quest fraught with risk. We can, however, usefully trace Thoreau's stance toward those aspects of his self and life which were sometimes obscure to him, which were sometimes deeply troubling, and, most important, which constitute the raw material out of which he constructed the narrators of his texts.

The attention paid to that narrator, as the epigraph from Michel Foucault suggests, must be linked with the knowledge that the author is dependent for his identity upon the same rules which govern the production of the texts. As much as meaning itself, the identity of Henry David Thoreau emerges for the readers insofar as we recognize a body of texts equated with that name. Following Foucault's logic, then, Thoreau is a literary figure that identifies a particular discursive practice arising in response to the nineteenth century's invention of psychological man. Rather than read Thoreau's work as the creative expression of a self developing over time, we perceive that author and text are produced by the discourse we recognize now as "Thoreau." Thus the analysis of this discourse must ask, in Foucault's words, "what is this specific existence that emerges from what is said and nowhere else?" Foucault's argument that discourse produces those objects which it appears to discover permits us to understand the genealogy of the authoritative narrator. It thus allows us to understand that the chaos of "Ktaadn" and the order of *Walden* do not negate each other. They mark, instead, the boundaries of the transformations possible within the discursive practice of idealism in nineteenth-century America.[1]

Thoreau's insistence upon the "I" in Walden has justified interest in the man among literary critics and cultural historians. Among psychologically oriented critics, the discussion has often been whether Thoreau's texts present "health" or "illness," a reading that necessarily equates narrator and man.[2] I argue, however, that the presence of psychologically revealing language—i.e., language that makes explicit what the modern age has found hidden in the depths of the self—does not necessarily implicate the presence in the text of a self struggling with its unconscious fears and desires. Guided by a progressive model of the world he found present in the self and in nature, Thoreau disdained any imputation of subjectivity and solipsism on his part. He insisted rather that the "perception of surfaces will always have the effect of a miracle to a sane sense."[3] Even his most personal writings are in no sense naive nor are they, in most cases, subject to verification by appeal to the memories and records of others. Instead, for Thoreau, "truth and a true man is something essentially public, not private."[4] The singular predicate should remind the reader that Thoreau ever strove to excise that which was personal and subjective. If we take Thoreau at his word and read the language of his writings for what it says and does rather than for what it refers to and means, his texts give us license to follow his intention in gaining a total mastery over what Schiller called "sense faculty"—for Thoreau, the information provided by the physical, the emotional, and the sexual.

We fail to recognize Thoreau's strategy for dealing with sex because we are accustomed to seeking it as it is hidden or repressed. Thoreau, however, solved what had become the problem of sexuality in the nineteenth century by making it a feature of the world rather than a constituent of the narrative self. That is, he accepted the terms of an age which problematized sex, but resisted its solution of silence and repression. He did so because he was aware that the existence of this self marked by depth and conflict contradicted his attempt to construct a narrator who spoke with authority. The sexual references and allusions in his prose have a purpose beyond that of frankness; they reveal sex (the entity discovered by the nineteenth century) to be a form of sexuality (the discourse in which it was produced). The narrator thus appears to discover in the world what he, the explorer of the self mirrored by that world, conquers. Thoreau denied sex the power to disturb by expressing in language what his neighbors and friends repressed in the self. In Thoreau's case, then, we must follow Foucault's advice about sexuality: "to account for the fact it is spoken about, to discover who does the speaking, the positions and viewpoints from which they speak, the institutions which prompt people to speak about it and which store and distribute the things that are said."[5]

Like the priest in the confessional and the analyst at the couch, Thoreau participates in a discourse of sexuality that places him in control by removing the narrator and interpreter of this discourse from it. The prevalence of sexual references in Thoreau's writing produces the true self—the narrator, the "I" of *Walden* and other works—insofar as he exists within a discourse that constitutes him as a figure of detachment from the disruptions of sex. The true self, Thoreau would have it, emerges from writing rather than existing prior to language.

The self of the historical Henry David Thoreau (or perhaps better, the self of David Henry Thoreau) was present only at the beginning of his literary career, awaiting the improvements of consciousness, language, and art until it was totallly metamorphosed into the speaker of the texts. For Thoreau, sexuality was not merely the expression of instincts and drives built into human biology. Since the culture in which he lived and worked presented sexuality as an "other" and thus as a problem to the Transcendentalists, the genius of his response was to include sexuality in his language, a strategy that both recognized the cultural dimensions of sexuality and gave his writing enormous power. The transition from the historical self to the ideal narrator depended, in large part, upon a deliberate revision of language that sexualized and materialized language as it desexualized and disembodied the self. This was Thoreau's psychological means toward his literary and philosophical goals, one guided by familiar transcendentalist concepts of the ideal nature of self and truth. His metamorphosis into the narrator is not just a rejection of the sexual and the physical, but also the repudiation of sensory experience as ontologically and epistemologically valid. Much, if not all, of the authority of Thoreau's narrators derives exactly from the process, hidden for the most part from the reader of his finished works, by which body becomes self, and self becomes narrator.

To achieve this end, Thoreau underwent a discipline through which bodily needs and sexual desire were transformed by the Reason of the poet. He was extraordinarily successful in this process of sublimation by which he sought to attain the permanence of the "sublime" in his own life and texts.[6] Even the frightening episode upon Mount Ktaadn, when bodies and physical nature apparently terrorize the speaker of that text, is an essential component of the decomposition of a self so that the narrator may be composed from the remaining and ideal elements. As an essay rather than the naive rendering of an experience, "Ktaadn" is less an unwilled and unwilling return of the repressed than a psychologically oriented critic might believe. It is, rather, testimony to Thoreau's success in relocating the physical and the sexual outside the speaker, a project he found necessary to continue to the very end of his writing. That is, a conflict between man and nature, replaced an internal conflict between mind and body.

II

There was a specific regimen by which sexual energy could be sublimated into the ideal and true; the word, which places the sublime in an abstract and nonthreatening realm, is essential for Thoreau. His references to the "streams" or the "waters" of life tend almost always to have a level of allusion that is directly sexual. In his journal, perhaps significantly just prior to the material he used in "Chesuncook," the second of the three essays that comprise *The Maine Woods,* Thoreau wrote: "When, after feeling dissatisfied with my life, I aspire to something better, am more scrupulous, more reserved, and continent, as if expecting somewhat, suddenly I find myself as full of life as a nut of meat . . . so I dam up my stream and my waters gather to a head."[7] Thoreau's punning on continent indicates the presence of more than simply upward displacement. The linguistic transformation from water to land and expression to containment envisions not only the redirection of sexual energy, but also its transformation, or perhaps more accurately, its reversion to the divine/natural energy that is its source and which is, in his terms, perverted by its use as sexual rather than ideal. References to his waters were present elsewhere in his literary career. In his 1844 essay on the abolitionist Nathaniel P. Rogers ("Herald of Freedom"), Thoreau had offered as his sole criticism this comment: "We would have more pause and deliberation, occasionally, if only to bring his tide to a head."[8] And the faith in damming up the waters of the self in order to come to a head remained with him: "In sickness and barrenness it is encouraging to believe that our life is dammed and is coming to a head, so that there seems to be no loss, for what is lost in time is gained in power. All at once, unaccountably, as we are walking in the woods or sitting in our chamber, after a worthless fortnight, we cease to feel mean and barren."[9] The language of sexual economy, like that of political economy, incorporated those truths which Thoreau believed in and relied upon. The truth of language guided his efforts in criticizing the conventional meaning and ordinary use of language and provided the *telos* for his life and writings. When, in *Walden,* Thoreau devised a series of metaphors and puns using the language of finance and the marketplace to describe his existence at the pond, he depended as well upon the power of sexual energy turned toward other and better ends. "I well nigh sunk all my capital in it"[10] is Thoreau's sexual and economic pun on the frustration and repression he thought it worthwhile to pay even if he did not think it worthwhile to mention the sexual here as directly and explicitly as the economic.

The enormity of that price was part of his reply to the aspersion that he was a parasite, an accusation he associated with unrestrained sexual expression. In his observations of nature he was particularly sensitive to parasites of all kinds, especially fungi. His remarks about them are revealing because the parasite and parasitical were exactly that which he rejected for himself and as a characterization of himself by others. Thus, a large toadstool "suggests a vegetative force which may almost make man tremble for his dominion"[11] because fungi were symbols of sexuality for Thoreau, natural erections neither restrained nor continent. He condemned the Maine loggers for their parasitical relationship with nature: their camps were "as completely in the woods as a fungus at the foot of a pine in a swamp."[12] Thoreau continued to criticize the loggers by identifying their assault on the woods as a form of sexual aggression: "No! no! it is the poet; he it is who makes the truest use of the pine—who does not fondle it with an axe, nor tickle it with a saw, nor stroke it with a plane."[13] The syntax and the verbs doubly damn the loggers, both for their sexual assault upon the wilderness and for the activity itself, which imposed upon nature uses and meanings alien to it.

Nature, however, sometimes presented the observer with a production thoroughly repellent and mystifying. He once found "a rare and remarkable fungus, such as I have heard of but never seen before."[14] The description and reaction make clear the relationship he perceived between sexuality and parasitism, and thus its opposition to Thoreau's scheme for his own life. "It may be divided into three parts, pileus, stem, and base—or scrotum, for it is a perfect phallus. One of those fungi named *impudicus,* I think. In all respects a most disgusting object, yet very suggestive."[15] What it suggested was ultimately confusing to one who sought from and in nature a sublime and asexual message: "It was as offensive to the eye as to the scent, the cape rapidly melting and defiling what it touched with a fetid, olivaceous, semiliquid matter. . . . Pray, what was nature thinking of when she made this? She almost puts herself on a level with those who draw in privies."[16] The question about nature's intentions was never answered directly. The fungus remained an anomaly and perhaps a warning should Thoreau's control over himself ever slip as to what the result might be— something "fetid" and "defiling."

Thoreau sought from nature a way to escape the pull of matter downward as he sought a way to translate the sexual energy of the erect penis into higher and better thoughts. A statement about friendship in *A Week* reveals the extent to which the transformation of body into mind pervaded his thinking, given the importance Thoreau attached to that relationship: "Friendship is not so kind as is imagined; it has not much human blood in it, but consists with a certain disregard for men and their erections . . . while it purifies the air like electricity."[17]

He desired not merely to control and restrain the body, but by means of language to eliminate physical necessity from his life and writings. His admiration for Sir Walter Raleigh, which he retained at least through the composition of *A Week,* was partially a consequence of Raleigh's ability to adjust to the most difficult of circumstances and triumph over them and therefore himself with language. He praised Raleigh's *History of the World* because it reflected an ability to turn

> his prison into a study, a parlor, and a laboratory, and his prison-yard into a garden, so that men did not so much pity as admire him—the steady purpose with which he set about fighting his battles, prosecuting his discoveries, and gathering his laurels, with the pen, if he might no longer do so with regiments & fleets—is itself an exploit. In writing the history of the world he was indeed at liberty; for he who contemplates truth and universal laws is free whatever walls immure his body.[18]

Thoreau felt that he had been born into that prison and that language alone remained as a weapon with which to do battle with his body and the world. He prefaced his comments on Raleigh's poetry with a thought on the importance and value of all poetry; it "lets us into the secret of a man's life, and is to the reader, what the eye is to the beholder."[19] The ideal quality of poetry was the same as that of nature, for both elucidated the self: "That is, man is all in all, Nature nothing, but as she draws him out and reflects him."[20] Thus Nature mirrors man; the true self is writ large in the natural world and the perception of the former in the latter validates the ideal essence of both in spite of sensory evidence to the contrary.

Thoreau contrasted the sex and parasitism of the historical self with the vocation of his narrative self. Thus, one of the major criticial traditions concerned with Thoreau has emphasized, to cite Sherman Paul, just how much Thoreau can be regarded as successful insofar as he "was to apply transcendental ideas, to bring them to the test of living—to embody them, to enact them, to realize them vocationally."[21] The first and last "problem" (Paul's word) was that of his own body: "I must confess there is nothing so strange to me as my own body. I love any other piece of nature, almost better."[22] The implied division of body from the rest of nature was tenable only insofar as it was the first step in the process of conquering all of nature: "The complete subjugation of the body to the mind prophesies the sovereignty of the latter over the whole of nature."[23] The faith in the progress of the mind in conquering the world was unalloyed by any skepticism or doubts in Thoreau's younger years. He dreamed of a complete and total victory: "Who knows how incessant a surveillance a strong man may maintain over himself—how far subject passion and appetite to reason, and lead the life his imagination paints? . . . By a strong effort may he not command even his brute body in unconscious moments?"[24]

Thoreau consistently used the language of war and the military to indicate how he might protect and conquer himself. He admired the soldier because he "is the practical idealist; he has no sympathy with matter, he revels in the annihilation of it. So do we all at times."[25] This imagery does seem to diminish during the middle years of his career and is especially faint in *Walden* in comparison with his other writings. The persona in that book is secure enough to discard armor visible to the reader; indeed *Walden* depends upon the acceptance by the reader that the narrator is "enabled to apprehend at all what is sublime and noble only by the perpetual instilling and drenching of the reality which surrounds us."[26] Still, the care and craftsmanship of *Walden* are products of the sentiments he had earlier expressed after a bout with bronchitis: "As soon as I find my chest is not of tempered steel, and heart of adamant, I bid good-by to these and look out for a new nature."[27] The same desire is present in *Walden*, albeit more tentatively and in language that retains and sublimates bodily and sexual energies for other and improved ends: "Yet the spirit can for the time pervade and control every member and function of the body, and transmute what in form is the grossest sensuality into purity and devotion."[28]

His idealism and dualism—"the blood circulates to the feet and hands, but the thought never descends from the head"—and the consequent revulsion from the physical and sexual attributes of man and nature permeate the language Thoreau used to describe the reformers of his day and his reaction to them.[29] He perceived them as explicitly sexual threats; they are portrayed as seductive individuals attempting to penetrate the armor Thoreau believed he needed to conquer the world successfully. The reformers "rubbed you continually with the greasy cheeks of their kindness. They would not keep their distance, but cuddle up and lie spoon-fashion with you."[30] Since the reformers themselves believed their appeal was to conscience and morality, this statement, while it may represent a genuine insight of Thoreau's, is just as clearly a projection of the historical self's fears and fantasies: "They lay their sweaty hand on your shoulder, or your knee, to magnetize you."[31] In *Walden,* Thoreau completed the projection so that the reader believes reform is a twisted sublimation of physical illness in the reformers: "If anything ail a man, so that he does not perform his functions, if he have a pain in his bowels even,—for that is the seat of sympathy,—he forthwith sets about reforming—the world."[32]

Unlike Thoreau, who sublimates and transforms the life inherent in sexual energy, the reformers are ironically described as mistaking their illnesses for ideas. The narrator is the disinterested and healthy observer, quite removed from the need and temptation to reform and from the dangers of being the object of reformation: "no doubt, he cures himself of his dyspepsia, the globe acquires a faint blush on one or both of its cheeks, as if it were beginning to be ripe, and life loses its crudity and is much more sweet and wholesome to live. I never dreamed of any enormity greater than I have committed. I never knew, and never shall know, a worse man than myself."[33] The narrator is the true reformer because he is able to swallow the world and expel that part which is waste material.

His perception of the progressive development of nature guided Thoreau's self-accusations. He found reassurance in the "slime" of nature because of what it produced: "How significant that rich, black mud produces the water-lily—out of that fertile slime springs this spotless purity."[34] However, nature was not always so teleological and comforting. Even though there were always times when he was perfectly the naturalist-observer, the attainment of such objectivity was itself cause for concern. As Thoreau found it more and more difficult to re-capture his earlier enthusiasm and mission, a question that had been a declaration of faith became instead a source of anxiety and lament: "What is Nature unless there is an eventful human life passing within her?"[35]

Thoreau was troubled by the very existence of independent functions within his own body that resisted or evaded being perfectly controlled, contained, and eliminated. A passage from the "Lost Journal" records his attempt to accept the body as distinct from and independent of control by the Reason:

> No man has imagined what private discourse his members have with surrounding nature, or how much the tenor of that inter-course affects his own health and sickness. . . .
> I am no more a freeman of my own members than of universal nature. After all the body takes care of itself—it saves itself from a fall—It eats—drinks—sleeps—perspires—digests—grows—dies— and the best economy is to let it alone in all these.

The best economy here seems to be that which is the title and subject of the first chapter of *Walden*. From the passage as al-ready given, we are aware that this body does not include sex-ual desire or procreation among its constituent functions. Even so, Thoreau found himself unable to "let it alone." Instead he sought to construct his "upper empire" by arranging the senses in a hierarchy of use, importance, and value and by applying that visual dominance and prospect to the self and nature:

> Why need I travel to seek a site and consult the points of com-pass? My eyes are south windows, and out of them I command a southern prospect. . . .
> The eye does the least drudgery of any of the senses. It oftenest escapes to a higher employment—The rest serve, and escort, and defend it—I attach some superiority even priority to this sense. It is the oldest servant in the soul's household—it images what it imag-ines—it ideates what it idealizes . . . In circumspection double—in fidelity single—it serves truth always, and carries no false news. Of five cast [e]s it is the Brahmin—it converses with the heavens.[36]

That visual dominance, so common among the American Tran-scendentalists, which found in the self and nature the same ideal truth and being, explains and structures Thoreau's repeated prospect experiences. They were designed less to test the self against nature than to metamorphose that self and body into the narrator who is always capable of viewing the world as if he "converses with the heavens." This hierarchy of body and consciousness shaped and transformed the experience of the self into the triumph of the narrator. It created a world in which consciousness, sublimation, the sublime, surfaces, narrator, and *Walden* followed from the discourse of sexuality, impulse, body, subjectivity, self, and "Ktaadn."

III

Thoreau had begun his writings with the conventional notions of this "southern prospect." In "Musings. April 20th 1835," which is perhaps the first of his "excursions," he chronicled the journey he had taken with his brother to that prospect from which they could survey the world below them and which included both nature and history:

> you suddenly emerge from the trees upon a flat and mossy rock which forms the summit of a beetling crag. The feelings which come over one on first beholding this freak of nature are indescribable. The giddy height, the iron-bound rock, the boundless horizon open around, and the beautiful river at your feet, with its green and sloping banks fringed with trees and shrubs of every description are calculated to excite in the beholder emotions of no common occurrence—to inspire him with vast and sublime conceptions.
>   The eye wanders over the broad and seemingly compact surface of the slumbering forest on the opposite side of the stream, and catches an occasional glimpse of a little farm-house "resting in a green hollow and lapped in the bosom of plenty," while a gentle swell of the river, a rustic, and, fortunately, rather old, looking bridge on the right, with the cloudlike Wachusett in the distance, give a finish and beauty to the landscape, that is rarely to be met with even in our own fair land.[37]

In this passage Thoreau used quotation marks to distinguish and differentiate himself from the merely conventional and banal; their presence asserts his superiority to the perception of others. But, significantly, to claim superiority through quotation does not reject either the aesthetic or the epistemological standards that attracted Thoreau to a scene he himself described in conventional and sentimental language. Thoreau's achievement is not so much as a naturalist who understood nature better as he grew older and learned more, but rather lies

in his ability to rewrite this particular scene and recreate this
particular world in language more sensitive to and aware of
both the world and the self observing it, in language that
showed the world and the self as mirrors of the other. He was
not then or ever opposed to many of the aesthetic and moral
values of his culture. Rather, to reiterate what both Thoreau
and his literary critics have already said, Thoreau made himself
into a man and writer who raised the quotidian and the trivial
into art by those values and that identity which his culture
presented to him.

In this description Thoreau claimed that the "boundless
horizon" and its attendant features evoked the emotions of the
sublime in him, even if he is reduced to the banality of "interesting" to label the world below. The young Thoreau placed his
sublime landscape away from his eye and at his "feet,"[38] indicat-
ing that the superiority of the observer was a necessary precon-
dition in order to recognize the sublimity of the landscape. The
desire to and the claim to be able to "inspire" the sublime derive
in part from Thoreau's rather special understanding of that
term. His essay, "Sublimity," assigned as a college theme by
Edward Tyrell Channing in 1837, reveals that particular usage
and, as well, the contentiousness of the college student.
Thoreau began his essay by quoting Burke on the sublime:
"Indeed terror is in all cases whatsoever, either more openly or
latently, the ruling principle of the sublime."[39] Thoreau was,
however, utilizing Burke to displace that quotation Channing
had originally assigned as the topic, which had derived sublimity from death. Unwilling at any time to consider death as a
source of meaning, Thoreau shifted the subject of the discourse by seeming to indicate that terror was a much better
basis for the sublime. He was not content to stop at this point
and continued by contending "we can hardly say that fear is a
source of sublime."[40] Instead Thoreau argued that the sublime
originated in the consciousness of the observer, aware of the
reverence due certain aspects of the world; therefore, only the
"calm and self-collected alone, are conscious of their sublimity."[41] If we recall the prospect in "Musing," we understand that
the "vast and sublime conceptions" arose because Thoreau's
linguistic control over the landscape was a product of his control over himself.

Thoreau had distinguished his concept of the sublime from
Burke's because he believed that Burke's "theory would extend

those emotions which the sublime excites, to the brute crea-tion."[42] Thoreau was speaking directly about animals, but he was implying much more about his relationship with his own body. The sublime was an ideal category whose existence he claimed to derive from the universal and natural law of the reverence due the superior by the inferior. The sublime was the measurement of the tribute the body pays the mind because the mind, in contrast with man's physical nature, aspires to and is capable of immortality: "In eternity there is indeed something true and sublime."[43] Only once in all of Thoreau's writings does he appear to put forward a different definition of the sublime. This occurs in "Ktaadn" when, after his experience on the mountain, he commented on the effect of traveling through the falls and rapids with such highly skilled guides as he had with him: "There was really danger of their losing their sublim-ity in losing their power to harm us."[44]

If there is a moment in which the material seems triumphant over the ideal, it is Thoreau's narrative of climbing and de-scending Mount Ktaadn. The report of this experience takes on added importance in context of Thoreau's repeated excur-sions to mountains. Thus, in his discussion of A Week, Lawrence Buell has remarked that "climbing a mountain was always a sacred act for Thoreau."[45] The narrative of Thoreau's journey up and his experience upon the top of Saddle-Back Mountain in A Week is both mystical and dramatic while his version of the expedition up and down Ktaadn is, if not the most dramatic writing, certainly the most melodramatic, calling attention to itself with the fragmented syntax, the italicized words, and the tone of terror which dominates it. Yet it must be considered more cautiously than it was by Leo Stoller in After Walden: "The universe pantheistically informed with a benign godhead had suddenly disassociated into its parts. For the rest of his life he was to strive in vain to reunite them."[46]

This judgment is too simple and easy for three reasons. First, Thoreau's intention in writing "Ktaadn" was to emphasize the wildness of the wilderness experience, as Robert C. Cosbey's examination of the manuscript has shown.[47] Second, Stoller, along with most other critics, paid no attention to the "seldom noted fact that Thoreau was working on "Ktaadn," the Week, and the first version of Walden all during his stay at the pond."[48] Third, and most important, to read "Ktaadn" in this fashion conflates experience and text, man and narrator. "Ktaadn" pre-

cedes *Walden* in more than chronological terms. Ontologically
and epistemologically it records disintegration of a self as part
of the composition of the narrator of *Walden*. Still, to reject
Stoller's formulation for these reasons is not to deny that
Thoreau's fictional self on the mountain in Maine differs
significantly from that of his previous narratives about mountains, and, in fact, appears to contradict them. He was to write
in *Walden*: "We can never have enough of Nature. We must be
refreshed by the sight of inexhaustible vigor, vast and Titanic
features."[49]

"Vast and Titanic" is the language descriptive of Ktaadn, to
which I now wish to turn. Thoreau divided the experience into
two sections; the first occurs as he climbs up almost to the
summit and the second consists of his "reflections" on the way
down. On the way up, the mountain is perceived as if it were
the "raw materials of a planet . . . which the vast chemistry of
nature would anon work up, or work down, into the smiling
and verdant plains and valleys of earth."[50] The concept of natural history as progressive is conveyed through language that
assumes a coming metamorphosis into the middle ground of
cultivation, consciousness, and poetry. But as Thoreau continues, the cloak of civilized and cultivated life is stolen: "Vast,
Titanic, inhuman Nature has got him at disadvantage, caught
him alone and pilfers him of some of his divine faculty."[51]

In the passage, nature changes from a mother to a stepmother, rejecting totally her unwanted charge: "Why seek me
where I have not called thee, and then complain because you
find me but a stepmother?"[52] With this rejection by nature, the
passage continues to grow in intensity:

> Perhaps I most fully realized that this was primeval, untamed, and
> forever untameable *Nature*, or whatever else men call it, while com-
> ing down this part of the mountain . . . we have not seen pure
> Nature, unless we have seen her thus vast, and drear, and inhuman,
> though in the midst of cities. Nature was here something savage
> and awful, though beautiful . . . It was the fresh and natural surface
> of the planet Earth, as it was made forever and ever,—to be the
> dwelling of man, we say—so Nature made it, and man may use it if
> he can. Man was not to be associated with it. It was Matter, vast,
> terrific—not his Mother Earth.[53]

The metamorphosis from wilderness to garden and material to
ideal can no longer be taken for granted. As Thoreau would
later state, there was an etymological, and hence real, link be-

tween wild and will.[54] His last words about Ktaadn were thus about the discovery of the wildness within himself:

> I stand in awe of my body, this matter to which I am bound has become so strange to me. I fear not spirits, ghosts, of which I am one—*that* my body might,—but I fear bodies, I tremble to meet them. What is this Titan that has possession of me? Talk of mysteries!—Think of our life in nature,—daily to be shown matter, to come in contact with it,—rocks, trees, wind on our cheeks! the *solid* earth! the *actual* world! the *common sense! Contact! Contact! Who* are we? *where* are we?[55]

In this passage it seems that consciousness has so transgressed its limits that the narrator will be unable to regain authority over nature and the self. But, in fact, the passage's stress on the sensory aspects of this experience effectually subverts a reliance upon the senses as a valid source of knowledge and identity. The loss of narrative composure at this moment is the loss of an identity Thoreau wished to discard upon Ktaadn.[56]

The experience that the will of this self was wild, beyond the control of his consciousness, was undoubtedly painful for Thoreau. He never climbed Ktaadn again although he returned to Maine twice and chronicled those expeditions in "Chesuncook" and "The Allegash and East Branch." In *A Week*, Thoreau had desired to climb Saddle-Back alone in order to reach as quickly as possible "such a country as we might see in dreams, with all the delights of paradise."[57] In "Ktaadn," he had hurried on before his companions seeking for himself the glory of penetrating "the hostile ranks of clouds."[58] But in "The Allegash and East Branch," he excused the omission of climbing the mountain "on account of the sore feet of my companion."[59] On Ktaadn, Thoreau jettisoned a narrative identity in an experience that is reminiscent of Poe's Arthur Gordon Pym's plunge into the arms of Dirk Peters and Ishmael's longing to fall from the masthead. But, unlike these experiences, Thoreau's apparent descent into the self is not a criticism of idealism. It records, instead, the rejection of that self's dependency on the material and the sensory.

On Saddle-Back, Thoreau had claimed to have discovered "the new world into which I had risen in the night, the new *terra firma* perchance of my future life. There was not a crevice left through which the trivial places we name Massachusetts or Vermont or New York could be seen."[60] About Ktaadn, he admitted, for perhaps the only time in his life and writings, that his significant opposition emerged from nature and his body rather than from man and society. The "vast advantage" of Saddle-Back metamorphosed into the "disadvantage" of Ktaadn. There has been some difficulty, much confusion, and little agreement among the critics who have attempted to reconcile this shift.[61] Since the narrative of "Ktaadn" is concerned with the disintegration of a self, this confusion may reflect the real difficulties presented by these texts.

Even the most devoted of his small band of disciples, Harrison Blake, apparently posed questions about the essay that were difficult for Thoreau to answer, all the more so because Thoreau was proud of "Ktaadn" as an essay. He wrote to Blake to explain how "Ktaadn" could be reconciled with what he had said and written elsewhere:

> Ktaadn is there still, but much more surely my old conviction is there, resting with more than mountain breadth and weight upon the world, the source still of fertilizing streams, if I can get up to it again. As the mountains still stand on the plain and far more unchangeable and permanent,—stand still grouped around, farther or nearer to my maturer eye, the ideas which I have entertained,— the everlasting teats from which we draw our nourishment.[62]

This letter was written over ten years after Thoreau climbed Ktaadn and suggests that he was not yet through rewriting the experience. Here the waters of life recur as "fertilizing streams," but transformed from physical and male into ideal and female. Still for all of the positive tone of the letter, its text is confusing with the implied division of nature into mother and stepmother—a fairy tale resolution indeed. The letter suggests that his experience upon Ktaadn presented an ongoing challenge to be continually recalled and defended. The apparent contradiction posed by the essay to the rest of his writings could *not* be dispensed with.

Thoreau needed Ktaadn and "Ktaadn" precisely because they confirmed the mind-body split he had already asserted in his catalogue of the senses and his prospect of nature. The journal entry for October 29, 1857 picks up this anxiety in recording that "such early morning thoughts as I speak of occupy a debateable ground between dreams and waking thoughts. They are a sort of permanent dream in my mind."[63]

The dream is as follows and its relationship to Ktaadn and other prospect experiences is striking:

> This morning, for instance, for the twentieth time at least, I thought of that mountain in the easterly part of our town (where no high hill actually is) which once or twice I had ascended, and often allowed my thoughts to climb. I now contemplate it in my mind as a familiar thought which I have surely had for many years from time to time, but whether anything could have reminded me of it in the middle of yesterday . . . I doubt. . . .
>
> My way up used to lie through a dark and unfrequented wood at its base,—I cannot now tell exactly, it was so long ago, under what circumstances I first ascended, only that I shuddered as I went along (I have an indistinct remembrance of having been out over-night alone),—then I steadily ascended along a rocky ridge half clad with stinted trees, where wild beasts haunted, till I lost myself quite in the upper air and clouds, seeming to pass an imaginary line which separates a hill . . . from a mountain, into a superterranean grandeur and sublimity.[64]

As in his essay on sublimity, Thoreau invokes horror and fear only to pass beyond them into the sublime. Like the lily that grows from the slime of the swamp, the pure truth of Saddle-Back emerges from the chaos of Ktaadn. That is, this "permanent dream" conflated the two modes of prospect experiences, Ktaadn and Saddle-Back, into one progressive model in which the ascent of Ktaadn and the disintegration of the self who climbed it are the necessary steps toward "superterranean grandeur and sublimity." Paradoxically, Ktaadn, although it occurred after Saddle-Back, affirms rather than subverts the earlier experience. Thoreau finally conquered Ktaadn and the wilderness by relocating them within his consciousness, by accepting a middle ground halfway between sleep and waking, and even death and life, for the mountain "rises in my mind where lies the Burying-Hill."[65]

When he wrote again to Harrison Blake, he drew for Blake the lesson of these mountain expeditions: "You must ascend a mountain to learn your relation to matter, and so to your body, for *it* is at home there, though *you* are not."[66] The acceptance of dualism is only provisional, as the letter continues, focusing more on the body than on external nature:

> Just as awful really, and as glorious, is your garden. See how I can play with my fingers! They are the funniest companions I have ever

found. Where did they come from? What strange control I have over them! Who am I? What are they?—those little peaks—call them Madison, Jefferson, Lafayette. What is *the matter*? My fingers, do I say? Why, ere long, they may form the topmost crystal of Mount Washington. I go up there to see my body's cousins. There are some fingers, toes, bowels, etc., that I take an interest in, and therefore I am interested in all their relations.[67]

Just at the moment when he claims a total victory over matter, body, and history, Thoreau sounds a bit hysterical. He achieved his victory at the expense—"I have sunk all my capital in it"—of sex and subjectivity. The violence of those narratives which refer to Ktaadn, whether directly or indirectly, marks the cost to human as well as external nature Thoreau believed he should pay to "improve" the self and the world.

Still there can be no doubt of his satisfaction with this triumph as there can be no doubt that the price he paid far exceeds that which his contemporaries and his readers admit either for themselves or Thoreau. In that same letter to Blake in which he had advised Blake to "ascend a mountain," Thoreau had once more reasserted his mastery over matter, his body, and the natural world:

> I keep a mountain anchored off eastward a little way which I ascend in my dreams both awake and asleep. Its broad base spreads over a village or two, which do not know it; neither does it know them, nor I when I ascend it. I can see its general outline as plainly now as that of Wachusett. I do not invent in the least, but state exactly what I see. I find that I go up when I am light-footed and earnest. It ever smokes like an altar with its sacrifice. I am not aware that a single villager frequents it or knows of it. I keep this mountain to ride instead of a horse.[68]

The abolition of the boundary between sleeping and waking, like the removal of the barrier between death and life, follows the transformation of the body and sexuality from the animate, the horse, into the inanimate, the mountain, which Thoreau can, as always, ride with ease. That "sacrifice" is of the identity which depends on the senses for its existence and validity. In its place is a self claiming to rely on "what I see"—I and eye are now one.

Thoreau's victory over mountains, over matter, and over his body was as complete as he wished. In a dream from which he had awakened with "infinite regret" to discover his body "a scuttle full of dirt," Thoreau had been dreaming of "riding, but the horses bit each other and occasioned endless trouble and anxiety, and it was my employment to keep their heads apart."[69] The narrator of "Ktaadn" differs from the narrator of *Walden* and Thoreau's other prose, but his discovery of matter and body *outside* the speaker is the necessary step by which the narrator of *Walden* and the other writings gained a voice the reader accepts as authoritative without perceiving it as either oppressive or repressed.

Notes

1. Foucault's discussion of the author and his replacement term, "author-function," is found in "What Is An Author?", in Michel Foucault, *Language, Counter-Memory, Practice: Selected Essays and Interviews*, ed. Donald F. Bouchard, trans. Donald F. Bouchard and Sherry Simon (Ithaca, N.Y.: Cornell University Press, 1980), pp. 113–39. Here, as elsewhere, my argument depends upon a radical questioning of the term *subject*, a project evident throughout Foucault's work. The quotation is from Foucault, *The Archaeology of Knowledge*, trans. A. M. Sheridan Smith (New York: Harper and Row, 1972), p. 28. Foucault takes up the issue of discourse itself most directly in *The Archaeology of Knowledge*, pp. 21–78, and in "The Discourse on Language," an appendix to *The Archaeology*, pp. 215–37. See especially his assertion that "the genealogical side of discourse" analyzes "the power of constituting domains of objects, in relation to which one can affirm or deny true or false propositions" (p. 234). The apparent contradiction between "Ktaadn" and *Walden* (the subject of the last section of this paper) can be best understood as one "localized only at the level of propositions and assertions, without in any way affecting the body of enunciative rules that makes them possible" (*The Archaeology*, p. 153). For the nineteenth century's construction of meaning within the discourse of organicism, continuity, development, and the "invention of man" as the being marked by these qualities, see Foucault, *The Order of Things: An Archaeology of the Human Sciences* (New York: Vintage Books, 1973), pp. 217–387, especially "The Organic Structure of Beings," pp. 226–32, "The Empirical and The Transcendental," pp. 318–21, and "Discourse and Man's Being," pp. 335–40. Of particular significance, given Thoreau's double focus on empirical fact and transcendental truth, is Foucault's observation that these categories emerge simultaneously with each other and with the appearance of "man" (p. 319).

2. Although it would be impossible to list all the critical work on Thoreau that uses as its means a psychologically derived theory and language or which takes as its end a psychological profile of the man, the following may serve to represent the vitality of this tradition: David Kalmen, "A Study of Thoreau," *Thoreau Society Bulletin* 58 (Winter 1948): 1–2; Raymond D. Gozzi, "Tropes and Figures: A Psychological Study of David Henry Thoreau," (Ph.D. diss., New York University, 1957)—a very influential Freudian study; Perry Miller, *Consciousness in Concord: The Text of Thoreau's Hitherto "Lost Journal" (1840–1841) together with Notes and Commentary* (Boston: Houghton Mifflin, 1958); Carl Bode, "The Half-Hidden Thoreau," in *Thoreau in Our Season*, ed. John Hicks (Amherst, Mass.: University of Massachusetts Press, 1962), pp. 104–16; Leon Edel, *Henry D. Thoreau* (Minneapolis: University of Minnesota Press, 1970); Michael West, "Scatology and Eschatology: The Heroic Dimensions of Thoreau's Wordplay," *PMLA* 79 (1974):

1043–64; Richard Lebeaux, *Young Man Thoreau* (Amherst, Mass.: University of Massachusetts Press, 1977); Eric J. Sundquist, *Home as Found: Authority and Genealogy in Nineteenth-Century American Literature* (Baltimore, Md.: Johns Hopkins University Press, 1979), pp. 41–85; Mary Elkins Moller, *Thoreau in the Human Community* (Amherst, Mass.: University of Massachusetts Press, 1980)—along with Lebeaux's book, this seeks to restore Thoreau to health and normality; and Leon Edel, "The Mystery of Walden Pond," in *Stuff of Sleep and Dreams: Experiments in Literary Psychology* (New York: Harper and Row, 1982), pp. 47–65—a revision of Edel's earlier work.

3. Bradford Torrey and Francis H. Allen, eds., *The Journal of Henry David Thoreau* (Boston: Houghton Mifflin, 1906), 4:313. August 23, 1852. Hereafter *J.*

4. *J*4:290. August 8, 1852.

5. Michel Foucault, *The History of Sexuality*, vol. 1, *An Introduction*, trans. Robert Hurley (New York: Vintage Books, 1980), p. 11. In calling attention to the distinction between sex and sexuality I am following Foucault's critique of "the repressive hypothesis" (pp. 17–49) in which he argues that one must account for "a veritable discursive explosion" since the seventeenth century.

6. In *Romantic Revision: Culture and Consciousness in Nineteenth-Century American Painting and Literature* (Chicago: University of Chicago Press, 1982), pp. 207–10, Bryan Jay Wolf discusses the importance of "naturalization" and "signification" in Thomas Cole's attainment of the "romantic sublime." Like Thoreau, Cole naturalized the "other" in order to be able "to confront directly the forces he must challenge (or which challenge him). . ." (p. 208). Wolf argues that the romantic artist did so by "hazard[ing] his identity for the sake of his goal (which is also his identity)" (p. 209). For Wolf, this new identity "frees the subject from his repressed attachment by sublimating desire, rerouting it along alternative pathways in a new psychic economy" (p. 209) as this identity becomes the "signifying term" in a new grammar of the self and world. My only quarrel with his description is that Wolf reads American Romanticism as a form of modernism; I would argue, rather, that the conventions and circumstances of nineteenth-century American culture set the terms of solution which Cole and Thoreau achieved.

7. *J*5:456. October 26, 1853.

8. *Reform Papers*, ed. Wendell Glick (Princeton, N.J.: Princeton University Press, 1973), p. 5.

9. *J*10:222.

10. *Walden*, ed. J. Lyndon Shanley (Princeton, N.J.: Princeton University Press, 1971), p. 17. Hereafter *W.*

11. *J*5:271. June 17, 1853.

12. *The Maine Woods*, ed. Joseph J. Moldenhauer (Princeton, N.J.: Princeton University Press, 1972), p. 19. Hereafter *MW.*

13. "Chesuncook," *MW,* p. 121.

14. *J*9:115.

15. *J*9:116.

16. *J*9:117.

17. *A Week on the Concord and Merimack Rivers*, ed. Walter Harding (New York: Holt, Rinehart and Winston, 1963), p. 232. Hereafter *A Week.*

18. "Sir Walter Raleigh," *Early Essays and Miscellanies*, ed. Joseph J. Moldenhauer and Edwin Moser with Alexander C. Kern (Princeton, N.J.: Princeton University Press, 1975), p. 197.

19. Ibid., p. 208.

20. *J*10:121. October 18, 1856.

21. *The Shores of America: Thoreau's Inward Exploration* (Urbana: University of Illinois Press, 1958), p. 16.

22. *J*1:321. February 21, 1842.

23. *J*1:487.

24. *J*1:79. May 21, 1839.

25. *J*1:135. April 22, 1840.

26. *W,* p. 97.

27. *J*1:214. February 14, 1841.

28. *W,* p. 219.

29. *J*1:204. February 7, 1841.

30. *J*5:264. June 17, 1853.

31. Ibid., p. 265.

32. *W,* p. 77.

33. *W,* pp. 77–78.

34. *J*5:283. June 19, 1853.

35. *J*5:472. November 2, 1853.

36. Perry Miller, *Consciousness in Concord,* p. 165. October 3, 1840.

37. *Early Essays,* pp. 16–17.

38. "Ktaadn," *MW,* p. 80. The one feature of prospect descriptions that remains present in all of his landscape writings is the formal division of the landscape into gentle and wild parts. After his experience on Ktaadn in Maine (discussed below), the narrator reestablished his control over himself and reasserted his aesthetics by calling attention to the "distant views of the forest from the hill, and the lake prospects, which are mild and civilizing in a degree" ("Ktaadn," *MW,* p. 80).

39. *Early Essays,* p. 93.

40. Ibid., p. 96.

41. Ibid.

42. Ibid., p. 97.

43. *W,* p. 96.

44. *MW,* p. 75. His usual judgment of the sublime was quite different. Just so far as man could master nature and matter, he would be in the realm of the sublime. As a college student, Thoreau had rather complacently considered the rapid commercialization of New England as a sublimation of the society:

> We glory in those very excesses which are a source of anxiety to the wise and good, as an evidence that man will not always be the slave of matter, but erelong, casting off those earthborn desires which identify him with the brute, shall pass the days of his sojourn in this his nether paradise as becomes the Lord of Creation ("Commercial Spirit," *Early Essays,* p. 118).

Although he may have come to doubt the wisdom of this praise for that activity, Thoreau's commitment to Transcendentalism itself follows from this division and conflict between mind and body.

45. Lawrence Buell, *Literary Transcendentalism: Style and Vision in the American Renaissance* (Ithaca, N.Y.: Cornell University Press, 1973), p. 221. See also Jonathan Bishop, "The Experience of the Sacred in Thoreau's *Week," Journal of English Literary History* 33 (1966): 73–76.

46. Leo Stoller, *After Walden: Thoreau's Changing Views on Economic Man* (Stanford, Calif.: Stanford University Press, 1957), p. 47.

47. Robert C. Cosbey, "Thoreau at Work: The Writing of 'Ktaadn,'" *Bulletin of the New York Public Library* 65 (1961): 21–30.

48. James McIntosh, *Thoreau as a Romantic Naturalist: His Shifting Stance Toward Nature* (Ithaca, N.Y.: Cornell University Press, 1974), p. 210.

49. *W*, p. 318.

50. "Ktaadn," *MW*, p. 63.

51. Ibid., p. 64.

52. Ibid.

53. Ibid., pp. 69–70.

54. *J*4:482; *J*9:450–51.

55. *MW*, p. 71.

56. Thoreau not only rejects Lockean philosophy here; his italicized "common sense" may well represent an attack on the Scottish Common Sense Philosophers who sought to manage and control the implications of Lockean thought by asserting the existence of a moral sense common to all.

57. *A Week*, p. 154.

58. *MW*, p. 63.

59. *MW*, p. 283.

60. *A Week*, p. 154.

61. James McIntosh has taken the moderate stance that Ktaadn represents "the possibility . . . that his relation with nature will fail" (*Thoreau as a Romantic Naturalist*, p. 205). For Leo Stoller, Ktaadn was the traumatic event of Thoreau's life (*After Walden*, pp. 45–47). Jonathan Fairbanks asserts that Thoreau's experience on Ktaadn "did not have to permeate every subsequent experience because it was not present in every subsequent experience." See "Thoreau: Speaker for Wildness," *South Atlantic Quarterly* 70 (1971):498. While Lewis Leary finds that Thoreau "carried the remembrance of it with him," he finally argues that the real meaning of Ktaadn for Thoreau resided in a "plea for conservation." See "Beyond the Brink of Fear," *Studies in the Literary Imagination* 7 (1974):76, 73. John G. Blair and Augustus Trowbridge offer the argument that Ktaadn so affected Thoreau "that he gradually formulated a distinction between the mountains . . . and the plains." See "Thoreau on Katahdin," *American Quarterly* 12 (1960):508. In "The Mark of the Wilderness: Thoreau's Contact with Ktaadn," *Texas Studies in Literature and Language*, 24 (1982):23–46, Ronald Wesley Hoag offers an argument that somewhat parallels mine in both its assertions and selection of quotations from Thoreau's writings. Where Hoag argues that man is the "true source of evil" (p. 23), I would demur and locate the genesis of evil not in "man" but in the historical self whose identity is found in family, culture, and society.

62. Walter Harding and Carl Bode, eds., *The Correspondence of Henry David Thoreau* (New York: New York University Press, 1958), pp. 491–92. August 18, 1857.

63. *J*10:141.

64. *J*10:141–42.

65. *J*10:143.

66. *Correspondence*, p. 497. November 16, 1857.

67. Ibid., pp. 497–98.

68. Ibid., p. 498.

69. *J*3:80. October 26, 1851.

Tennyson's Fables of Emergence

Timothy Peltason
Wellesley College

T ENNYSON'S relations to Romantic poetry have quite properly been the focus of much recent investigation of his poetry, and there has been little difficulty in establishing the Romantic basis of what may be called Tennyson's philosophy: of his fundamental agnosticism, that is, and of the consequent emphasis in his poetry on questions of epistemology and on the situation of consciousness in the world. I want to participate in this conversation, but also to enlarge it, by looking at two very different early poems, "The Kraken" and "The Lady of Shalott," different in tone and style and achievement, but joined nevertheless by their allegorical treatment of the difficulties that attend the emergence of the self into the world.[1] In their focus on the act of emergence, these poems make oblique comment on the perils that confront any self that would make its entry into the world, but especially on the situation of the young poet who would emerge into the light of contemporary and literary history as well as into the paradoxically constricting, yet enabling realm of language. And in the very obliqueness of that comment, these poems represent an important and purposeful Tennysonian modification of Romantic lyric form, a modification that recasts the separation of the self from the world as a separation of the poet from the enclosed space of his own poem. This separation, accomplished by the manner of the poems, is commented on by their matter, by their account of the act of emergence as difficult, dangerous, fatal. Yet matter and manner together also constitute the distinctive form of Tennyson's presence in his poems and make possible his own emergence as a new poetic voice.

As every reader since Harold Nicolson has noticed, Tennyson's poems, especially those written before the death of Arthur Hallam, examine again and again situations of abnormal isolation and inwardness, as well as the usually frustrated struggle to emerge from such situations. But this drama of engagement and withdrawal, in the finest and most characteristic of Tennyson's early poems, is enacted not by the poet himself, but by his creations. Instead of a strong first-person singular whose interests and activities we are encouraged to identify with those of the poet, these unconversational poems present fabulous, or at least fictional, creatures whose careers are surely, but obscurely, representative of the poet's own human and artistic concerns. The result, in poems like "The Kraken" or "The Lady of Shalott," or like "Mariana" or "The Dying Swan" or "The Lotos-Eaters" or many others, is a kind of instant mythology. But these myths are not authorless and impersonal. Instead they join an intensely lyrical and personal style to their oddly impersonal structures, so creating evocative stories or situations that are obviously the product and yet not obviously or explicitly the self-expression of the poet who stands behind them.

Yet Tennyson is hardly self-effacing; his poems are forthrightly Tennysonian. It is rather that he diffuses or divides his presence, appearing at the center of the story, in the disguised form of the fabulous beast or lady, and also as the distinctive and resourceful voice who brings the story to us. This voice, however, discourages intimacy even as it affirms the personality of the poet, for Tennyson's style is personal in the manner of Milton, in this celebrated account by T. S. Eliot: "Milton's style is not a classic style, in that it is not the elevation of a common style, by the final touch of genius, to greatness. It is, from the foundation, and in every particular, a personal style, not based upon common speech, or common prose, or direct communication of meaning."[2] Applied to Tennyson, this distinguishes him not only from the metaphysical and modern poets whose rougher rhythms Eliot was in general concerned to vindicate, but from the authors of what M. H. Abrams has named the greater Romantic lyric. In this descriptive-meditative form, the distinctive lyric instrument of Wordsworth and Coleridge, Shelley and Keats, style *is* based on the direct communication of meaning and of the experience of the poet-speaker who is the chief actor in his own poem. But Tennyson acts in his own poems only through speaking, seeming to give way entirely to his fictional representations. This being so, it is natural that critics have described Tennyson's style, but have chosen generally to interpret only his stories, to discover the meaning of "The Lady of Shalott" solely in the career of the lady of Shalott, to let her be the artist of the piece. But such interpretations leave out of account the hidden protagonist and the chief interest of the poem, the language-maker himself, whose attempt to enter the world may have taken a different form and achieved a different result from that of his creations. The problem of emerging from isolation and from a painfully mediated relationship with the world, is one that the lady of Shalott shares with her creator, and both their stories must be examined.

I

First, however, there is "The Kraken," a poem from Tennyson's first adult volume, the *Poems, Chiefly Lyrical* of 1830, the account of a fabulous sea beast whose existence is stranger and even more strangely abbreviated than that of the lady of Shalott. In his unimaginably long life, the kraken emerges from his sleep for only one equivocal instant. If "The Lady of Shalott" is Tennyson's most extended and most explicit fable of emerging selfhood, then "The Kraken" is surely his most condensed and darkly intimate, remaining for most of its fifteen lines in the submerged and subconscious depths:

> Below the thunders of the upper deep;
> Far, far beneath in the abysmal sea,
> His ancient, dreamless, uninvaded sleep
> The Kraken sleepeth: faintest sunlights flee
> About his shadowy sides: above him swell
> Huge sponges of millenial growth and height;
> And far away into the sickly light,
> From many a wondrous grot and secret cell
> Unnumbered and enormous polypi
> Winnow with giant arms the slumbering green.
> There hath he lain for ages and will lie
> Battening upon huge seaworms in his sleep,
> Until the latter fire shall heat the deep;
> Then once by man and angels to be seen,
> In roaring he shall rise and on the surface die.[3]

Like the lady of Shalott, the kraken pays for his emergence
into the world with his life, and, like the lady of Shalott, he has
hardly a life at all, just a long, dull sleep and single burst of
roaring glory. This abysmal life and fiery death may have their
reasons, but the poem says nothing of them and offers no
prominent interpretive handles, no tapestries or whispered
curses. It is a powerful descriptive fancy, but an oddly impersonal one. A critical approach that seeks to trace in lyric poems
the career of an ego seemingly has no entry. Tennyson's own
note refers the reader to the *Natural History of Norway* by Bishop
Erik Pontoppidan, but this arcane source furnished him with
nothing more than a name for his beast. Tennyson would have
read of the kraken in other places, too, in Scott's *Minstrelsy* and
T. C. Croker's *Fairy Legends,*[4] and his language of apocalypse
derives, of course, from the book of Revelation. But none of
these "sources" renders the poem's vague but insistent evoca-
tions less vague, or helps us to determine just what sort of
performance it is.

One alternative is to forget about egos and to take the poem
instead as the career of an id, a career of gross animal indulgence called finally and justly to judgment. The repressed
urges of the deep self burgeon in darkness until the whole
system overheats, and these urges are expressed to the surface
and exposed to view. Any source-hunting, then, is for the dark
sources of human personality, which are as unfathomable and
undiscoverable as the origins of the kraken himself or the bottom of his ocean. The poem cannot tell when or how the kraken was born, or even precisely where he lies now. His place is
rather defined by its distance from other places, below an "upper deep," "far, far beneath," but, curiously, the ocean's floor is
never named, and no bottom is set to this inwardness.

"The Kraken" is not quite an allegory of the hidden, instinc-
tual self, but it surely permits a glimpse of some inner region,
and that such a region should be unfathomably dark and deep
sorts well with the received image of Tennyson as a brooding
and introspective youth. But there is something, too, in the
poem that is out of keeping with all this profundity, and some
other region of the poet's self that must have acted in its making. Although the poet cannot have been present at the scenes
he describes and so has no place in the history of the kraken, he
puts his mark on that history, nonetheless, in the rich and particular forms of his language. The sense of a richness that

builds to excess in the poem comes not just from the imagined luxuriance of undersea vegetation, but also from the confidently playful manipulation of an extravagant and rich-sounding descriptive vocabulary. The poem may shudder at the kraken and his fate, but it clearly delights, too, in its own language, and presents evidence of a poet who is young and brilliant, steeped in Milton and Shelley as well as in ancient beast lore. The poet writes of something strange and distant, but at the same time announces to the responsive reader his own eager English talent.

Is "The Kraken," then, merely a youthful tour de force, in thrall to its author's reading and ready abilities and to a vaguely profound sense of the submerged self? Every poem, after all, must be written, and we can always distinguish, even when such distinctions are discouraged, between the subject or speaker and the working poet who stands behind them. But "The Kraken" heightens this distinction: first, and most obviously, by doing without the fiction of a speaker who would mediate between poet and poem; second, and more remarkably, by the strangely mingled dark and light of its tone. There is no purposeful blending, as we might expect in a poem of such seeming inwardness, of the experiencing consciousness within the poem and the shaping consciousness who writes it. Instead, the two are kept apart, and the poem seems oddly divided, a dark and portentous fable on one reading and an exuberant invention on another. A third, more adequate, reading can go beyond this division only by discovering its significance, and this, in turn, will depend on a demonstration that the fable is more than just dark and portentous and that its inventor intended more than exuberance.

The second demonstration is easy enough, for exuberance clearly fails to account for all the technical resources of the poem, which go far beyond the matching of a luxuriant diction to a luxuriant scene. Both Christopher Ricks and W. David Shaw have written well about the way in which the odd rhymes and the carefully controlled rhythms of the poem enhance its portrayal of a long, slow life and a precipitous death.[5] Another evidence of conscious design and of the fitness of design to theme is the characteristically innovative form of the poem, a fifteen-line sonnet whose extra line is over stuffed by an extra beat. The story that the poem has to tell extends and exceeds its ordinary limits just as the kraken rises to the limit of his world

and passes fatally beyond it in the poem's last line. Such effects
are the results of a sophisticated and complex artistic intention,
an intention which can be recovered only through elaboration
of the fable in which it realizes itself.

One possible reading would have the kraken a poet figure
arising from the gloom of obscurity into the dangers of public
exposure. This is the image suggested by the notice that Tennyson and his brothers attached to their first volume in 1827: "We
have passed the Rubicon and we leave the rest to fate, though
its edict may create a regret that we ever emerged 'from the
shade' and courted notoriety."[6] Such a reading would conform
with Tennyson's notorious sensitivity to adverse criticism, as
well as with the poem's implicit acknowledgment of hidden and
shameful impulses, impulses that the poet might well be shy
about bringing before the public in any but the disguised form
of a fable. But to the degree that "The Kraken" describes or
suggests the emergence of repressed matter, it discourages
further inquiry, for how can the poet do more than suggest the
shape of fears and feelings that are hidden from himself? The
subconscious processes that the poem invokes are the object of
the poet's articulate and conscious concern. A reading that respects both the inwardness and specificity of the fable must
consider the form in which the poet emerges out of himself and
into public view; on this reading, the kraken is a poem in the
making and "The Kraken" is an allegory of poetic composition.

"Tennyson's surface, his technical accomplishment, is intimate with his depths."[7] Read as an allegory of poetic composition, "The Kraken" illustrates and criticizes this remark by T. S.
Eliot. Surface and depth are properties that we attribute not
just to persons, but to poems, and it is the relationship between
poetic surface and personal depth that "The Kraken," both in
its form and in its fable, puts in question. The argument for an
intimate relationship must rest on the readiness with which we
connect the poem's purely descriptive and external language to
a psychological and inward condition. But the connection is all
ours to make, and the fable, with its assertion of a necessary and
fatal separation between surface and depth, suggests the
difficulty and the uncertainty of any penetrations of the surface. The kraken dies, and men and angels know him only as a
corpse.

But neither the kraken nor "The Kraken" begins at the surface, and the allegory of poetic composition can be mapped out in more detail only by returning to the depths:

> Below the thunders of the upper deep;
> Far, far beneath in the abysmal sea,
> His ancient, dreamless, uninvaded sleep
> The Kraken sleepeth. . . .

The poet begins with an act of imaginative penetration, the only way possible into the depths of the sea or of the self. But his act has its limits, and the kraken's sleep remains uninvaded and his origins unimagined. No truly original moment or place can be fixed for the act of poetic composition, which arises from the negativity of silence, darkness, distance, and profound unconsciousness. The phrase "Far, far beneath" is reminiscent of the "Far, far away" that haunted Tennyson from earliest boyhood.[8] The late poem entitled "Far, far away" uses the phrase to bind together past and present, but in a way that suggests not a recovery of origins, but the naming of an original absence. Even when the poet can transport himself back to his earliest memories they are memories not of wholeness and presence, but of what was already the distance of longing. "The Kraken" does not strike quite this emotional note, but it does seek the origins of poetry in a strange and distant place, only to find them hidden still in a distant time.

The kraken himself, however, does not care where he comes from or what he does without. So great is his passivity that he seems almost the object and not the agent of his own sleep. Yet things are happening in the murky depths. Some light penetrates; the "huge sponges" suggest absorption, ingestion, and anticipate the kraken's own unconscious feeding on huge sea-worms. The creature of the mind that is destined to become a poem begins its life in unconsciousness. Thus the moment usually conceived as creative and original, when the unconscious form first rises into consciousness, is actually preceded by long gestation. The raw materials of the poem—be they experience, knowledge, other poems—have been absorbed unconsciously over an indeterminate period. These are the bits and pieces that will be transformed in the finished poem, a fragment from Pontoppidan's history grafted to an image out of Revelation. The line that describes the actual feeding—'Battening upon

huge seaworms in his sleep"—itself feeds upon both Milton and
Shelley. "Battening" is a piece of poetic diction that Tennyson
had surely read in "Lycidas" and in *Prometheus Unbound,* 4,
l. 542, where Demogorgon calls to the "Elemental Genii" who
reside even in "the dull weed some sea-worm battens on." Battening upon the seaworms in his turn, Tennyson's kraken in-
habits a familiar region, but represents a new link in the chain.
In making a poem, the poet both absorbs and enters a tradition.

The expressive and active phase of poetic composition, then,
is part of a larger movement, relying both on a history of passivity and reception and on the extraordinary impulse from the
world without that provokes one phase into the next. An external pressure catalyzes the kraken into fulfilling what has always
been his destiny. "In roaring he shall rise and on the surface
die." In this single, grand, full-voiced and mythical moment the
poem is a living and conscious form, aimed at the world without. This great outpouring of voice has a clear place in the
poetic process, but what is the death at the surface? If the
surface marks the boundary between inward experience and
the publicly available forms of language, then the relationship
between the poet and his poem is discontinuous, and the kraken's death is a figure for the death of the poem into language.
The living intention of the poet assumes its fixed and bodily
form in the language of the poem, but his body is immediately a
corpse. Like the dead body of a once-living creature, the language of the poet is clearly *his,* and just as clearly not *him.*

But the poem does not linger in mourning over the kraken
any more than it pauses to explicate his story or to complain of
the superficiality of language, its distance from the deep concerns of the poet. Instead it installs this distance as a feature of
its own design. "The Kraken" is confessedly a made object, in
mediated relationship with the world of experience, and in this
it follows the model for poetry that it allegorically presents. The
time between the kraken's feeding and his emergence implicitly
acknowledges the belatedness of the poem relative to anything
outside itself that it might seek to describe or repeat. And the
evident literariness of the poem, its reliance on other texts,
acknowledges the necessary indirection by which the poet must
find the language of inwardness in sources outside the self. Not
only time, but the language of other texts, mediates the relationship of the poem to the experience of the poet.

Mediation appears in the fable as the absolute discontinuity of death, the death of the kraken that establishes emphatically the failure of connection between the realms within and without the sea of consciousness. The surface of the sea marks a limit, the point at which experience dies into language, but also the point at which the language of the poem dies into external experience. The poem must end when confronted with the world outside its sea of consciousness, a world it cannot represent. Either way, the effect is to enforce the separation of language from experience. Self and nature, the mighty opposites of Romantic poetry, are absent from "The Kraken," for its mode is neither mimetic nor expressive, nor some combination of the two. The descriptive-meditative lyric of the Romantics has yielded to a form that claims neither function, but that is lyrical nonetheless, the singular record of a singular sensibility. For Tennyson's poetic language does assert its power and place in the world, if not through its ability to announce the presence of a human speaker or to refer directly to his experiences of the world, then through its clear evidences of a human poet and through the allegorical intention that I have attempted to document. "The Kraken," to the precise extent that it signifies a discontinuity between poetry and experience, is relevant to the experience of the poet, both dependent upon it and able to say something about it. And the scrupulous indirection of this saying is the sign of the poem's self-awareness and self-containment. But "The Kraken," though it is detached, is hardly cool or unconcerned. Its youthful poet masters a difficult subject, but not by minimizing the difficulty or condescending to it. Urgent matters are in question, and other poems, under pressure of greater emotional agitation, will struggle harder against the necessity of mediation and acknowledge more regretfully the limitations of the speaking self.

II

In turning to "The Lady of Shalott," we turn to an ampler performance and one for which there exists already a tradition of allegorical interpretation, a tradition that has arisen in response to the poem's evident, but provocatively unspecified, relevance to the activities of the poet. A few critics, it is true, have declined to burden this "gossamer fancy" with gross meanings,[9] but most have followed the poet's own lead, in his contribution to Canon Ainger's *Tennyson for the Young,* and given the lady an allegorical function.

> The new-born love for something, for some one in the wide world from which she has been so long secluded, takes her out of the regions of shadows into that of realities.[10]

Interpretations have grown longer and more ingenious, but seem always, like this one, to have achieved coherence through the suppression of insistent details of the poem. This account forgets to explain why "reality" in the poem does nothing for the lady except kill her. She lives under the shadow of a curse that retains all its potency when she leaves the shadowy realm. The curse has been variously interpreted, most often as the poet's vocation, rightly enforcing his isolation from the world. In this reading, the lady errs in coming out, even if the error is one with which we can sympathize. Again, however, some details are suppressed, and we must wonder if she would have erred less in staying in. That she is caught in a hopeless situation seems clear at the first mention of the curse:

> There she weaves by night and day
> A magic web with colours gay.
> She has heard a whisper say,
> A curse is on her if she stay
>   To look down to Camelot.
>
> [ll. 37–41]

The double emphasis of "stay" here perfectly reflects the lady's dilemma. The regularity of meter and the insistent rhyme scheme force the reader to emphasize "stay" and for a moment to take the thought as complete. A curse is on her, presumably, if she stays where she is, in her isolated tower.

Even with the next line the curse might be taken as proscribing the continued isolation from which she merely looks down on the world. Of course, the second and commonly accepted reading of the passage is that made clearer by the 1832 version:

> No time hath she to sport and play:
> A charmed web she weaves alway.
> A curse is on her, if she stay
> Her weaving, either night or day
>   To look down to Camelot.

The ambiguity of the passage, as revised, underscores the ambivalence of the lady's situation, for she, like the kraken, really has little to choose. The two are alike, as Christopher Ricks has noted, in moving from one sort of death to another.[11] One might, with certain local adjustments, repeat for "The Lady of Shalott" the allegorical reading of "The Kraken" above. The lady, as poetic conception, begins her career within the brain. Ricks notes the influence on the poem of several passages from Spenser, notably from the account of Britomart's mirror in *The Faerie Queen,* Book 3. A little further in the background might be the tower chambers of the House of Temperance in Book 2, which represent the chambers of the mind. The mind receives and records sensory impressions of the world without, until, under the pressure of some external event, the lady-poem emerges. The poem is even signed, as the lady signs her boat, but once again there is a death to pay for the passage into currency, and the lady has fallen, as the kraken rose, into language. This reading has at least the advantage of avoiding an inappropriate judgment of the lady's action. She is neither right nor wrong in coming out, but only true to a destiny that requires her to inhabit first one realm, then another. Yet clearly, far more than in the case of "The Kraken," the allegory of poetic composition leaves a great deal unaccounted for. Other significant details and allusions insist on being interpreted. Even more, the evident human pathos of the poem resists reduction to purely linguistic terms, however important language is to the poet. It does not seem likely that any reading will be satisfactory that translates the straightforward poetic narrative into a straightforward critical narrative. The poem's narrative *is* straightforward and describes a single action, but the critic must retell the story in many ways, if he is to be adequate to the resonances with which Tennyson has informed the lady's exemplary act of emergence.

Written around this act, the poem assumes and enforces a necessary opposition between inside and outside. In "The Lady of Shalott," as elsewhere in Tennyson, the world seems divided into these two problematically related realms. And for the lady, as for Mariana and so many others, relations with the world "outside" are severely restricted. Until her fatal decision, she never truly sees the outside world, but instead, an interior image of it:

And moving through a mirror clear
That hangs before her all the year,
Shadows of the world appear.
There she sees the highway near
  Winding down to Camelot:
There the river eddy whirls,
And *there* the surly village churls,
And the red cloaks of market girls,
  Pass onward from Shalott.
                    [ll. 45–53, emphasis mine]

Why the mirror's "magic sights" (l. 65) are magic is uncertain, but they are suspect on this account, mere "shadows," and they are untestable. The reader is never given an opportunity to compare what appears in the mirror with some more authoritative narrative perception. Suspicion arises from the change wrought in the landscape by the lady's emergence. The sunlit perfections of the earlier scene yield to gloom directly on the mirror's breaking:

In the stormy east-wind straining,
The pale yellow woods were waning,
The broad stream in his banks complaining,
Heavily the low sky raining
  Over towered Camelot.
                    [ll. 118–22]

One cannot know if it is the world or merely the lady's image of it that has been transformed. Nor, for that matter, can one know if the distinction is meaningful or possible. The world of sound has changed as well, or rather, it has been discovered on leaving the "silent isle" (l. 17). The "silent nights" (l. 66) of the lady's habitual experience become the "noises of the night" (l. 139) as she travels down the river. In the 1832 version the lady hears the tinkling of a sheepbell (l. 48), but this is excised in revision. Until Lancelot's entry, she has heard nothing except a whisper of uncertain origin, and even when Lancelot does appear the lady as hearer and viewer is strangely elided. Part 3 of the poem begins by taking the reader out of the tower enclosure, "A bow-shot from her bower eaves" (l. 73), but the lady cannot come along. The ensuing sights and sounds are given the reader directly by the narrator, without the interposition of the lady or her mirror. Only after the long description does Lancelot appear to the lady:

> From the bank and from the river
> He flashed into the crystal mirror,
> "Tirra lirra," by the river
> Sang Sir Lancelot.

[ll. 105–108]

We assume she hears the song, because immediately after this she takes her decisive action. The song itself is hardly a message, but only a few nonsense syllables. Yet the mere fact of its reaching, or seeming to reach, the lady directly from outside is sufficient to mark this critical juncture in the poem. For the lady's dilemma, or one version of it, is her imprisonment in the world of self and the seeming impossibility of real contact with the world beyond. The poem draws on a long literary tradition of imprisoned damsels who must be liberated, but the figures of the evil jailer and the heroic, aggressive suitor are absent. The lady is held by no more than a whispered curse and is wholly unknown to Lancelot until after her death. The self has only itself, both to enforce isolation and to rebel against it. This imprisonment is the condition described by Walter Pater in his conclusion to *The Renaissance*.

> Experience . . . is ringed round for each one of us by that thick wall of personality through which no real voice has ever pierced on its way to us, or from us to that which we can only conjecture to be without. Every one of those impressions is the impression of the individual in his isolation, each mind keeping as a solitary prisoner its own dream of the world.[12]

The Lady of Shalott begins, like Pater, resigned to this cloistered life, to the inner activity that Pater goes on to characterize with an image taken from Homer, but reminiscent of Tennyson, as "that strange weaving and unweaving of ourselves." The lady, as the poem opens, has not yet conjectured to be without the world. When this happens she turns to the world and takes her decisive steps. That the poem pictures such a turning need not be an assertion of its possibility. The poem as fiction imagines the emergence from self into unmediated contact with the world, but in so doing it must quickly end, for it can imagine only the enigma of death. That both kraken and lady die on entry into the world outside may be read as a confession from Tennyson that the world beyond the self is finally as mysterious as the world beyond the grave.

Yet, in some sense, the mystery of the world is more haunt-
ing, because both more subtle and persistent, than that of
death. Men know that they know nothing of death and are glad
to have little contact with it, but the external world seems always
present and dissolves only under analysis. So the Lady of
Shalott senses the world in her mirror and is satisfied with it
until some extraordinary event or impulse causes her to see her
shadows for what they are and to conceive a desire for more.
She becomes suddenly aware of the world as an absence, aware,
in Pater's terms, that she is "without" something. To examine
"The Lady of Shalott" as a treatment of the discovery of desire
broadens discussion and brings more of the poem into focus.

The discovery of desire is, among other things, the discovery
of time, for only in time can desire pursue its object or imagine
its fulfillment. If the self wants something that it does not have
now, it must posit a then, past or future, as the time when the
wished-for object was or will be made present. For the Lady of
Shalott, as her poem begins, there is only now. Her stillness at
the center of a moving world is emphasized by the opening
description. A landscape dominated by the linearities of road
and river is organized "Round an island there below, / The
island of Shalott" (ll. 8–9). People move continuously up and
down the road, while on the river "The shallop flitteth silken-
sailed" (l. 22). This recalls the shallop and the "silken sail of
infancy" from the opening lines of Tennyson's 1830 "Recollec-
tions of the Arabian Nights," where the waterway is explicitly
named as "the forward flowing tide of time." The opening
image of "The Lady of Shalott" is of continuing, active life, an
image that is only reinforced when one notices that the traffic is
all going in one direction. Everything is "Flowing down to
Camelot" (l. 14) or "Skimming down to Camelot" (l. 23) or
making its way there by some other means. In contrast to this
directed activity the "Four gray walls and four gray towers"
(l. 15) of the lady's enclosure are oriented in no particular direction, and their only activity is to "overlook" some flowers.
Verbs, in the lady's isolated realm, are intransitive and denote
motion without locomotion:

> Willows whiten, aspens quiver,
> Little breezes dusk and shiver
> Through the wave that runs forever
> By the island in the river
>   Flowing down to Camelot.

[ll. 10–14]

It is a single wave, infinitely repeated. Indeed, all actions, on and off the isle, seem mere repetition when viewed from the lady's unique vantage. Until the end of part 2, the poem employs an habitual present tense to describe the actions that appear in the lady's mirror "sometimes" (l. 55) or "often" (l. 66). No action is unique.

Then mood and tense change in the pivotal closing stanza of part 2:

> But in her web she still delights
> To weave the mirror's magic sights,
> For often through the silent nights
> A funeral, with plumes and lights
>   And music, went to Camelot;
> Or when the moon was overhead,
> Came two young lovers lately wed;
> "I am half sick of shadows," said
>   The Lady of Shalott.
>
> [ll. 64–72]

This is a single sentence, but it covers a distance thematically and grammatically and takes several odd turns. It begins in the present tense and shifts, without clear grammatical warrant, to the past at "went"; funerals "often" went to Camelot, making this, perforce, an habitual past tense. It is not clear, though, whether young lovers came by from their weddings often or only once. If often, then why suddenly with such dramatic effect? Or is it the lovers alone who have the effect? The function of the connectives "for" and "or" is vague, and this vagueness blurs the causal structure of the sentence. "For" asserts that the funerals are a reason why the lady "still delights" to weave. "Still" is double, too, reminding of the lady's immobility, but chiefly telling that the lady continues to delight in her weaving even though "She hath no loyal knight and true," which was the final assertion of the preceding stanza. The funeral is a reason for her continued delight, perhaps because it is a visually stimulating spectacle, more persuasively because it is an emblem of the mortality that the lady avoids by her removal from life. Grammatically, "or" ought to introduce another reason for the lady to delight in her weaving. Yet it is immediately linked, if only by contiguity, to her expression of dissatisfaction, "I am half sick of shadows." This is an oddly decisive moment, odd because she is only half sick after all, but still decisive because it is the lady's first utterance, and with it the poem shifts abruptly to describe a succession of unique events that emerge as a vector from the circle of habitual actions that have come before. The poem has moved into the flow of time, which now moves inexorably toward the lady's death.

The wedding and funeral, as images of generation and death, appropriately accompany the shift from the lady's timeless retreat to the world of temporal progression. They are the bitter and sweet of a life in time. The lady is only half sick of shadows, one guesses, because she wants only half the bargain. Half, however, is sufficient to draw her wholly out of her protective cell and into the world. The impossibility of going only halfway is amply demonstrated when the lady turns in desire to look upon Lancelot and her mirror and web are immediately destroyed. Once turn to the world and there is no turning back, or, put another way, once realize the enigma of the self's position in the world and time, and there is no return to unconscious acceptance of life and one's place in it. As soon as the lady has become half sick of shadows, she has recognized an absence in her world and thus embarked on the project of desire. Her desire is for Lancelot, or at least for the bonding she has seen in the married couple and even in the knights riding two and two. Lancelot's ringing "bridle bells" pun on "bridal" and call to the lady as a promise of fulfillment. Quite suddenly, her world is not enough and she is driven outside to seek there her completion. To leave the prison of self behind and truly join with another would be to redress that grievance that Mariana suffered in her moated grange and that Yeats later characterized as "the perpetual virginity of the soul." We may believe with Mariana that such an ideal is unattainable, but why, in the terms of this poem, must the search for it lead so directly to the lady's death?

Part of the answer lies, no doubt, in the poem's association of the funeral with the wedding. The lady must accept death as the wages of life. Birth and growth lead inevitably to death, but it seems somewhat harsh that they should lead immediately to it as well. The lady's death, like the kraken's comes hard on her emergence into life.[13] In the vertical action of the fable, time is collapsed and the end terms, death and birth, are brought together. This is an extreme image for the commonplace insight that, in the world of temporal succession, the end is inherent in the beginning. Yet our reading should not be too literal. This near coincidence of the lady's figurative birth and actual death does not represent a shortened life-span so much as a heightened consciousness of mortality. In like manner, the lady's emergence does not necessarily signify her emergence into time, but her emergence into consciousness of time. All people are always implicated in the flux of time; the lady's original removal was merely her protective unconsciousness of this fact. As the lady's emergence is actually the figure of an operation of consciousness, so is her death. What is truly lost, and thus what is immortalized in the lady's death, is the present moment, the *now*. It was all the lady had before, and suddenly it is precisely what she lacks. The lady's continuous weaving had earlier been the guarantor of her safety from time. By weaving always what she saw, she was kept firmly focused on the present moment. Imagination did not enter in. There was no opportunity to think of what was not. Then, as Lancelot flashes into view, the present is lost in the rush of desire. The lady leaves off her weaving of the perpetual moment and turns to pursue fulfillment in the course of a temporality that has suddenly opened around the present and into the flux of which she is drawn. This is the experience of time that Pater describes elsewhere in his conclusion to *The Renaissance:* "all that is actual in [time] being a single moment, gone while we try to apprehend it, of which it may ever be more truly said that it has ceased to be than that it is." With the lady's turning, the poem enters history and shifts to the past tense.

That this loss of the present is related to the operations of desire is clear in the passage that describes the lady compelled into action:

> She left the web, she left the loom,
> She made three paces through the room,
> She saw the water-lily bloom,
> She saw the helmet and the plume,
>   She looked down to Camelot.
>
> [ll. 109–113]

The verbs here carry an extraordinary force that is the effect of their uniqueness in the poem. For the first two lines the lady is the active subject in the process of putting things decisively behind her. More strikingly, this sense of activity persists through the next two lines, in which "saw" describes an act of appropriation. These lines suggest the voraciousness of perception, the way in which the lady uses things up, exhausts them by seeing them once.[14] The lady is suddenly in time, embarked on

a career of recklessly progressive action, or at least on what
passes for recklessness in her limited world. To satisfy her sudden appetite for the world, she looks upon it and so enters into
that active pursuit of experience which renders experience
paradoxically ungraspable. This is the state of being that Tennyson earlier described in "Timbuctoo:"

> . . . even then the torrent of quick thought
> Absorbed me from the nature of itself
> With its own fleetness.
>
> [ll. 138–40]

This dizzying experience helps to explain the desire, frequent in Tennyson, to expand a single moment and to hold
time still. Yet this leads to the stasis that is also a fearful spectre.
The burden of a time that passes but has nowhere to go Tennyson explores elsewhere, in "Mariana" and "Tithonius." The
only reliable fact about time in Tennyson's world is that it is
never what one wishes it to be.

What Tennyson and his creations wish for most characteristically is a recovery of "the days that are no more." If fulfillment
is always elsewhere, it is not always in the future, for desire is
twinned with memory and Tennyson's poetry, under the
shadow of Wordsworth, cannot evade the past and must confront repeatedly the regressiveness of desire. "Ulysses" and *In
Memoriam* are the great and sustained investigations in Tennyson of a need to move forward that is also a need to return, and
even in "The Lady of Shalott" we can discern the regressive
impulse, Tennyson's own hearkening back to the moment just
before the onset of his career in the world and time. But desire
predominates over memory as an explicit subject matter in this
poem about starting the world, and this betrays the presence of
a nearer influence than that of Wordsworth.

Shelley is, preeminently, the poet of Romantic desire.
Similarities between "The Lady of Shalott" and "The Witch of
Atlas" have been noted by Lionel Stevenson, who remarks in
both poems a lady who weaves and then emerges from seclu-
sion for a magical boat ride.[15] "Alastor" seems yet a closer relative, for it is there that Shelley most clearly charts the fatal
course of desire. Thomas Weiskel has written that "romantic
desire, as everyone knows, can never be fulfilled. It is as fundamentally narcissistic as romantic memory, for the object, the

'some other Being,' of each is a displaced projection of the present which contains within it the insufficiency of that present." He goes on to observe of "Alastor" in particular that "at just the point where 'objects cease to suffice,' the insatiate mind responds to its anxiety of deprivation . . . by projecting and consolidating a 'single image' of the Other."[16]

The quest's true object is the identity of the pursuing subject with the objective self. The subject is the vessel of desire, hurried forward through time seeking a coincidence with some less fleeting version of itself. For the Lady of Shalott, if not for Shelley's protagonist, this would mean returning to where she started. The discovery of time is the discovery of the struggle to transcend it. This reading not only reveals the regressive character of desire, but questions the sincerity of the desire to get beyond the self. There is hardly room for Lancelot in the process we have described. Tennyson repeats a Shelleyan formula in "The Lady of Shalott," but he also criticizes it by his different treatment. Shelley's questor is a heroic, if doomed, figure, who pursues through several continents and 700 lines a creature confessedly the product of vision or dream. The lady, in contrast, succumbs almost immediately to her fate, never truly seeking Lancelot except in death. She is a compromised figure, not to be admired without qualification. The reason for this lies partly in Lancelot's separate existence. For the lady, it is perhaps true that the life of things and people outside the self is as mysterious and uncertain as the life after the death, but the reader is granted another perspective. Unlike the Being of the vision in "Alastor," who presumably dies with her suitor, Lancelot survives the Lady of Shalott to pronounce the valediction:

> He said, "She has a lovely face;
> God in his mercy lend her grace,
> The Lady of Shalott."
>
> [ll. 169–71]

To use Lancelot against the lady in this way is not to make him out an admirable figure. His treachery in the Arthuriad is a part of his presence in any poem, and we are made to sense throughout the heedlessness of his manner. The "Tirra lirra" that he tosses off kills the lady before he is even aware of her existence, and his final words, though touching, are pointedly inadequate. He is, nonetheless, another human being, and it is the lady's fatal weakness that she can do no justice to this fact, but only discover in his image the vacancy of her enclosed self. Yet she is not to be damned, for the insistent possibility exists that her weakness is that of every person. The poet hopes not, however, and he inscribes that hope obscurely in the form of his poem, which struggles simultaneously to be an objective narrative and an act of communicative self-expression.

We come, finally, to a reading of the poem as an allegory of literary history and of the ways in which literature accommodates the problem of human separateness. The lady begins, as Aristotle says that a poet should, by holding a mirror up to life. The tapestry that she makes is, in etymological fact, her text, from the Latin *texere,* "to weave," and it is a text in the high mimetic mode. The lady stands apart from the object of her imitation and thinks to weave exactly what she sees, without pausing to examine the assumption of privilege this involves. Her prison of subjectivity appears now a prison of objectivity, or rather an emblem of the poet's delusion of objective stance. Far from being a removal from everyday life, this repeats precisely the error of that life, the assumption that we are able to see things as they are, and that to render this vision as the naively mimetic artist does is an unproblematic affair. The images of mirror and web confess the mediation that is involved both in seeing and in recording what one sees, but the lady does not at first question this enforced distance from all around her.

"Down she came" (l. 123); the lady's emergence has generally been read as a descent into the quotidian, the move, in Tennyson's terms, from shadows to realities. The equivocal status of these terms ought, however, to be clear upon reference to Plato's allegory of the caves from Book 7 of *The Republic,* a text echoed in Tennyson's repeated use of "shadows" to denominate the mirror's reflections, and in the images of fire and sunlight that characterize the realm without. The events of daily life, in Plato's allegory, are the events of the cave. The life of custom is the world of shadows in which the lady begins. The lure of reality, keeping to Plato, is not the lure of normal human relationship, but of higher vision. So the lady, as artist, moves in the course of the poem from a conventional imitative art into the realm of visionary poetics.[17] Her emergence is a rejection of the mediation of appearances, an effort to "see into the life of things," in Wordsworth's phrase. This involves, too, a rejection of the pose of objectivity. Emergence into the world signifies an admission of the subjectivity of all perception. This moves beyond Plato to the Romantic recognition that the self is implicated in the discourse of perception and cannot stand apart. To look on nature or the world is to interact with it.

For both Plato and the Romantics, the realm of vision is the realm of light, and Lancelot is insistently associated with things light and sparkling. Sun dazzles and flames on him, his shield sparkles, his bridle glitters like stars. The central image is of fire: "The helmet and the helmet-feather / Burned like one burning flame together" (ll. 93–94). These are the two details of Lancelot's appearance that the lady sees when she turns away from her mirror—"She saw the helmet and the plume"—just as fire, in Plato's allegory, is the first light seen by the cave-dwellers when they break from their shackles. The fire over Lancelot's helmet recalls also the Pentecostal tongues of flame that appear over the heads of the Apostles to signify the gift of a new speech. The lady is drawn from her shadows to Lancelot's light in a movement that finally recalls Wordsworth's visionary gleam—the lady is later a "gleaming shape" (l. 156)—the light of Romantic imagination.

Yet there is a paradoxical loss of light when the lady comes out and encounters the gray, rainy skies. Why should the light be lost just as it is sought? The discussion of desire suggested one answer. The allegory of literary history suggests another. The lady, as Romantic poet, has lost sight of the gleam. External nature fails to provide the light it once provided. If the loss seems to come early in the lady's career, we recall that Wordsworth was already in his teens writing poetry that lamented the loss of nature's inspiration and that Tennyson in his twenties had read Wordsworth. Tennyson observes nature minutely in his poetry, but rarely makes even the pretense of consulting it as a privileged text. Instead he took this first step in his reading and learned from the Romantics that human meanings must be created, rather than discovered. But he learned, too, that such creation may prove fatal, and, in "The Lady of Shalott," it is not only nature that fails. The lady in her boat becomes a "bold seer in a trance" (l. 128), a true visionary thrown back on her own resources, as were the Romantic poets. But she fails:

> And down the river's dim expanse
> Like some bold seer in a trance,

> Seeing all his own mischance—
> With a glassy countenance
> Did she look to Camelot.

She can see her failure here, and the mirror that she meant to leave behind reappears in her "glassy countenance," likely a pun on "glass" as mirror and so an assertion that she can only reflect light, that she must stand second to something. Were her soul truly a lamp, her story might end differently.

As it is, she dies, and in her death floats slowly down to Camelot and public view. In the 1832 version of her poem she bears a stark message on a parchment:

> *The web was woven curiously*
> *The charm is broken utterly,*
> *Draw near and fear not—this is I,*
> *The Lady of Shalott.*

[ll. 168–71]

"This is I"—it is the most straightforward act of self-presentation. Or not quite the most, for that is reserved for the 1842 version in which the lady presents simply herself with no word at all, save her signature on the boat. She does sing "a carol mournful, holy / chanted loudly, chanted lowly," but this is a mere melodic exhalation, the sign and substance of the elegiac consciousness that is the only fruit of her entry into life. The kraken rose and died "in roaring," and the lady here dies "singing in her song," an oddity of phrasing that makes the song explicitly and literally a vehicle of self-presentation.

We are back to the lady as poem, but with a significant change. She did not begin as a poetic impulse, but as a poet. Her transformation is a self-imposed reduction. The poem describes the passage from a naively mimetic conception of art to an extreme and equally naive conception of art as self-expression. Activated by the dual realization that art must be subjective and that normal experience is mediated, the lady, as English poetry, overreacts. This is Tennyson's critique of a poetry that seeks to abandon all mediation, whether in the interest of observing a Presence in nature behind its appearances, or of presenting the self directly. The lady's rejection of all language, her launching of herself into the world, is a hyperbolic version of the rejection of poetic diction in the effort to become in poetry merely a man speaking to men. This

Wordsworthian project, or rather Tennyson's fundamentalist and interested version of it—less a reading of Wordsworth's poetry than of his program and also a recognition by Tennyson of his own deep temptations—is criticized by Tennyson on two grounds: first, because the mediating screen of language will never become truly transparent and disappear; second, because the poetry of unbridled self-expression leads dangerously to self-expenditure. The lady's last song, like the swan's death hymn to which it is compared,[18] is an exhalation of life. The image recalls Keats's nightingale "pouring forth [its] soul" in song. It is too much, as the abbreviated careers of all the Romantic poets (even Wordsworth, whose poetic death by this time would have been clear) would have seemed to Tennyson to confirm. But he does not recommend a return to the artistic values of the lady's weaving. In the course of literary history, as in the course of desire, there is no turning back. If neither of the lady's options is acceptable, however, then what does the poem offer? It offers, of course, itself.

There is, first, the interesting confusion about the poem's turning point. The obscurities of causation in the long closing sentence of part 2 are part of a larger, conscious strategy to undercut the pretensions of any single turning point and to diffuse the lady's moment of decision. In that long sentence it was not clear whether the mention of the funeral, with the shift into past tense, or the lovers (who may have come often, or just once), or neither, marked the poem's turning point and motivated the lady's "I am half sick of shadows." Likewise, there is the "half" that qualifies that moment and makes us look to several others as possibly more crucial. The assertion of the preceding stanza, "She hath no loyal knight and true," may seem to mark the real beginning of trouble for the lady, the fact from which the rest of the poem inevitably proceeds. Immediately after the lady's assertion the stanza breaks and the poem leaps an unspecified gap in time, from moonlight to sunlight at least. The appearance of Lancelot seems to mark another new beginning and leads to another climactic moment, or sequence of moments, when Lancelot flashes into the mirror, sings his "Tirra lirra," and obliges the lady to turn from her weaving and so bring down the curse.

Each of these moments claims some privilege, offering itself as potentially crucial, and between the first and the last of them is interposed the portrait of Lancelot. He is traveling to

Camelot, but a few striking images suggest the possibility of a suspension in midmotion: his shield, for instance:

> A red-cross knight for ever kneeled
> To a lady in his shield
> That sparkled on the yellow field,
>   Beside remote Shalott.
>
> [ll. 78–81]

The echo is of Spenser, but a closer analogue is the lover perpetually about to kiss his beloved on Keats's Grecian Urn. In both images stasis eternalizes desire and guards it against exhaustion. Yet the shield for all its sparkle is as cold as the urn. A better solution is the near stasis that only seems to stop time, as in this description of Lancelot's bridle.[19]

> The gemmy bridle glittered free,
> Like to some branch of stars we see
> Hung in the golden Galaxy.
>
> [ll. 83–85]

With this image the poem has it both ways, or pictures the possibility of having it both ways, as Lancelot seems to exist both in and out of time.

In its diffusion of a critical moment into several moments, the poem repeats this possibility in its own form. The lady's decisive act of emergence is actually several acts at several narrative moments, arranged around the portrait of Lancelot with its images of suspended motion. The apparent confusion about the moment of passage from one realm to another thus represents the possibility of an extended liminal moment, a space and time somehow in between the lady's two undesirable alternatives. This extension would seek to redress several related grievances. The drastic foreshortening of life that has seemed to characterize the ritual of emergence in both "The Kraken" and "The Lady of Shalott" obliges just such an attempt to extend the precariously brief interval between birth and death. This possible space between the lady's two negative fates suggests also a middle road for poetry between the extremes of a pseudo-objective mimesis and the vain striving for a self-expression that puts away all mediation.

The lady's double curse, then, is the mediacy of language, which the poet seemingly cannot do with or without. The middle road that "The Lady of Shalott" seems to suggest is an

acceptance of the belatedness of language, its failure of immediacy. This would correspond to the period of the lady's period of *half*-sickness, in which she knows her world's inadequacies but has not moved vainly to correct them. The past tense of the second half of the poem purposely counters the lady's struggle against mediation. It is thus the poem's own explicit confession of its belatedness relative to what it describes: accept this failure of presence, the poem seems to say, and the poem can begin its restituting labor of re-presenting. The stanzas on Lancelot enact this sequence. He first appears to the reader for thirty-odd lines and only then flashes into the lady's mirror. This re-presentation is thus a repetition that extends the moment of Lancelot's appearance. If repetition is secondary, it is also preservative. That more may be lost than preserved is the necessary risk. Doing without the mirror altogether is impossible. The temptation to which the lady finally succumbs is twofold. She sees Lancelot in the mirror and she hears his voice. The mirror image she sees is oddly doubled. It comes "From the bank and from the river" (l. 105). This reflection of a reflection is an image of the lady's own secondariness that she cannot abide. Lancelot's melody offers an allied temptation. It is the lure of primacy, of language regressed to inarticulate song. To know one's secondariness and abide it is the poetic courage that "The Lady of Shalott" advocates.

"The Lady of Shalott" and "The Kraken" are both cautionary fables about emergence, exposing the difficulties and the dangers facing the self that would make its debut. Yet at the same time they are exemplary acts of emergence, announcing the presence of a strong, new poet. Acutely aware of his place in literary history, of the lessons of Romanticism both positive and negative, Tennyson sustains this tradition in the only way possible, by embracing mediation as a resource, even while accepting it as a curse. The poet emerges in these poems powerfully, but indirectly, and this indirection is the mark of a new self-consciousness about the properties of language.

I do not claim this self-consciousness as a superior virtue or a proof of enlightenment, but merely as a fact of Tennyson's artistic psychology and of literary history. Indeed, Tennyson does not stay convinced of either the adequacy or the necessity of this particular form of self-consciousness. But for now and in these poems, the uncertainty of language as a vehicle of emergence and communion is the obsessive concern of the poet's labor. For language, in the vocabulary of my discussion of "The Lady of Shalott," is neither "inside" or "outside." When called on to describe moments of inwardness, language is dismissed as belonging to the realm of things: "Matter-moulded forms of speech" is the phrase from *In Memoriam*. Yet for description of the world of external, historical experience, language is apparently too personal and subjective. And this ambivalence of language both permits and requires of the poet his new obsession. The opposition between the worlds inside and outside the self yields to an opposition between the worlds inside and outside the poem, between language and all the forms of experience that it may seek to represent. Expressive and mimetic theories founder on the same shoal. Tennyson, however, is not content to rest with a nonreferential concept of language, for in a poetry without extralinguistic meanings the poet himself has no place. Such a poetry is not unthinkable, but it is not Tennysonian either, for his is not the way of austerity, but of intense personality and distinctive voice. Voice announces a human presence in his most characteristic early poems, even as the poems themselves refuse to portray the human agent of this voice. This strange reticence, strange in a poet so obviously and obsessively personal as Tennyson, compels a more active reading. "The Lady of Shalott," though it rejects a naive construction of mimetic or expressive art, struggles to be both, to tell of the world and of Tennyson's own experience. The kraken dies at the surface, but there is one equivocal moment—"once by man and angels to be seen"—when he may be glimpsed as a living form. The struggle of interpretation as I have practiced it in this essay is to glimpse the poet in his moment of emergence: not any longer an actual moment, but rather the uncertain presence through the text of the poet striving to realize himself obliquely in the form of language. Reading the poetic allegory as revelation of self, the reader attempts to hypostatize the moment of becoming and assert a continuity between self and language. But his assertion must, of course, be renewed with each reading of the poem, and there remains as well the potentially greater threat to the integrity of the self that is posed by its engagement with the world of time.

The true discovery of time is the discovery of the radical shifts in perspective that experience can compel, and the author of "The Lady of Shalott," for all his interest in sudden ruptures, has at least one hard lesson still to learn about the dramatic discontinuity of experience. Tennyson, in writing "The Lady of Shalott," achieved more than his lady, but suffered less. I have argued that Tennyson's scrupulous indirection in these early poems is a measure of poetic strength, self-knowledge, and control. The mythological treatment of the pains of selfhood preserves a distance from its subject, a distance that it calls inevitable and names as part of the difficulty of experience. But the embowered and melancholy self, sending off its messages in the form of beautiful glass bottles, is about to discover new and painful connections with the world beyond. Its enclosure, which once seemed the problem of problems, will be all too readily violated by the fact of death. Losing Arthur Hallam, Tennyson suddenly finds himself standing outside his old subject, in sudden need, but also in sudden and urgent possession of a new expressive idiom. Losing Arthur Hallam, Tennyson loses all the hard-won distance from existential difficulty that made his first great poems possible, and discovers at a blow the subject of his mature poetry.

Notes

1. I use the term *allegory* loosely here, but it nevertheless seems like the right one. I have in mind the tantalizingly interpretable quality of both these poems, the sense that their real significance is just out of reach and can be grasped only when we learn how to translate their fabulous stories onto some other plane of discourse. And I have in mind also Paul de Man's special use of the term in his influential essay "The Rhetoric of Temporality" (in *Interpretation: Theory and Practice,* ed. Charles S. Singleton [Baltimore: Johns Hopkins, 1969], pp. 173–209). For de Man, the allegorical is distinguished from the symbolic as the properly Romantic mode of language, the mode of language that knows its own unlikeness from the world to which it may seem to refer and with which it can never truly coincide. De Man's account of a language that knowingly separates itself from the world is clearly relevant to my readings of "The Kraken" and "The Lady of Shalott," although I ultimately wish to distinguish this de Manian Romanticism from Tennyson's practice.

2. T. S. Eliot, "Milton II, " in *On Poetry and Poets* (New York: Farrar, Straus, and Cudahy, 1957), p. 175.

3. I quote Tennyson from Christopher Ricks, ed., *The Poems of Tennyson* (London: Longmans, 1969).

4. This information is helpfully collected by Ricks in his headnote to "The Kraken."

5. Christopher Ricks, *Tennyson* (New York: Collier, 1972), pp. 44–45. W. David Shaw, *Tennyson's Style* (Ithaca, N.Y.: Cornell University Press, 1976), pp. 76–77.

6. *Alfred Lord Tennyson: A Memoir by His Son* (New York: Macmillan, 1897), 1:22.

7. T. S. Eliot, "In Memoriam," in *Critical Essays on the Poetry of Tennyson,* ed. John Killham (London: Routledge and Kegan Paul, 1960), p. 215.

8. Charles Tennyson, *Alfred Tennyson* (New York: Macmillan, 1949), p. 25.

9. Stopford Brooke, *Tennyson: His Art and Relation to Modern Life* (London: Isbister, 1894), p. 128.

10. Quoted in *Memoir*, 1:117.

11. Ricks, *Tennyson*, p. 45.

12. Walter Pater, *Works* (London: Macmillan, 1900), 1:235.

13. For an interpretation of the lady's emergence as an image of birth, see W. D. Paden, *Tennyson in Egypt* (Lawrence, Kans.: University of Kansas Press, 1942), pp. 155–56.

14. An allied account of perception is Emily Dickinson's "Perception of an object costs / Precise the objects's loss." The passage is cited and discussed by Denis Donoghue in *The Sovereign Ghost* (Berkeley, Calif.: University of California Press, 1976), pp. 128–29.

15. Lionel Stevenson, "The 'High-Born Maiden' Symbol in Tennyson," in John Killham, ed., *Critical Essays*, pp. 129–30.

16. Thomas Weiskel, *The Romantic Sublime* (Baltimore, Md.: Johns Hopkins University Press, 1976), pp. 144–45.

17. See also James Hill, who argues that the poem represents an advance from an Appollonian to a Dionysian conception of poetry: "Tennyson's 'The Lady of Shalott': The Ambiguity of Commitment," *Centennial Review* 12 (1968): 415–29.

18. In ll. 136–41 of the 1832 version.

19. Harold Bloom refers, in *Poetry and Repression* (New Haven, Conn.: Yale University Press, 1976), p. 152, to Tennyson's use of "the most characteristic of the Keatsian metonymies, which is the substitution of a near-stasis or slow-pacedness for the language of the sense, for the sounds and sights of passing time."